E-Leaders

Peter Cohan

T0341874

- Fast insight into earning hard currency profit from the Internet

- Covers the key areas of the pyramid of Web business models, nine Internet business segments and six core concepts for profiting from the Internet

- Examples and lessons from some of the world's most successful e-leaders, including GE, Dell, Cisco Systems and NTT DoCoMo, and ideas from the smartest thinkers, including Tim Berners-Lee, Marc Andreesen, Robert Metcalfe, Vint Cerf and Michael Mandel

- Includes a glossary of key concepts and a comprehensive resources guide

LEADING
08.03

First published 2002 by
Capstone Publishing (A Wiley Company)
8 Newtec Place
Magdalen Road
Oxford OX4 1RE
United Kingdom
http://www.capstoneideas.com

CIP catalogue records for this book are available from the British Library and the US Library of Congress

ISBN 1-84112-232-7

This book is printed on acid-free paper

Substantial discounts on bulk quantities of Capstone books are available to corporations, professional associations and other organizations. Please contact Capstone for more details on +44 (0)1865 798 623 or (fax) +44 (0)1865 240 941 or (e-mail) info@wiley-capstone.co.uk

Contents

Introduction to ExpressExec

ExpressExec is 3 million words of the latest management thinking compiled into 10 modules. Each module contains 10 individual titles forming a comprehensive resource of current business practice written by leading practitioners in their field. From brand management to balanced scorecard, ExpressExec enables you to grasp the key concepts behind each subject and implement the theory immediately. Each of the 100 titles is available in print and electronic formats.

Through the ExpressExec.com Website you will discover that you can access the complete resource in a number of ways:

» printed books or e-books;
» e-content – PDF or XML (for licensed syndication) adding value to an intranet or Internet site;
» a corporate e-learning/knowledge management solution providing a cost-effective platform for developing skills and sharing knowledge within an organization;
» bespoke delivery – tailored solutions to solve your need.

Why not visit www.expressexec.com and register for free key management briefings, a monthly newsletter and interactive skills checklists. Share your ideas about ExpressExec and your thoughts about business today.

Please contact elound@wiley-capstone.co.uk for more information.

Introduction to E-Leaders

What is the Internet and how does it fit into the history of economic development? Why is the Internet important? How can businesses profit from the Internet? What are the risks and opportunities inherent in investing in the Internet, including:

» what distinguishes a technology leader from its peers; and
» what distinguishes the performance of the technology leaders.

The Internet has proven itself to be the most significant economic and social phenomenon of the latter half of the 1990s and the early 2000s. The financial markets have been replete with tales of investment killings made in a day, simply by appending ".com" to a company's business model. One of the oddest of these is the story of Zapata Corporation, a fish protein company started by a former US President, whose stock doubled in a day when it announced that it was spinning off its Internet business. And since April 2000, trillions of dollars' worth of stock market value related to such economic forces has been destroyed.

To managers and investors schooled in the notion that the value of a company is related to its future profits, the Internet is a perplexing phenomenon. So many of the publicly traded Internet companies have scant revenues and substantial net losses. Why then are these companies worth so much more than many other companies that are much larger and earn substantial profits? In asking this question, managers and investors are struck with two conflicting emotions. One emotion is the desire to get a piece of the Internet action. The other is a nagging fear that the whole thing is a house of cards that is doomed to unravel at some unspecified point in the near future.

The purpose of *E-Leaders* is to cut through these emotions to get at the reality of the Internet phenomenon. *E-Leaders* is not another exhortation to large companies about why they need to put their businesses on the Web. Nor does it elucidate 10 new economic principles received from a trip to the top of Mount Sinai. *E-Leaders* is about the companies that are working to make economic sense of the Web. It is about understanding the underlying dynamics of the industry segments in which these companies compete. It is also about a search for the business strategies that distinguish the market leaders from their peers.

In thinking about these questions, it is interesting to take a look at something that happened 100 years ago. In the 1890s, oil was discovered in Titusville, PA. Hundreds of independent drillers rushed to the site to get their share – but as more oil was introduced into the market, the price fell dramatically, wiping out all but the most well-capitalized drillers.

Into this boom and bust cycle strode John D. Rockefeller. He saw that the industry could not survive unless there was a way to damp down these wild fluctuations in supply. So Rockefeller began investing in refineries, which were one of the key choke points in the oil industry. Refineries would buy crude, process it into salable end-products, and then find a downstream market for the result. But refineries were only one part of the system that needed to be brought under control. If a driller or refiner produced a commodity but couldn't move it to the market, that commodity had no value.

Rockefeller therefore began exerting his power to fill up railroad cars with a steady supply of oil products, and using that power to negotiate volume discounts on railroad transportation. It was worth it to the railroad barons to give Rockefeller a discount on transportation costs in exchange for the profitability of a fully packed train. The result was an industry perfectly engineered to provide cheap energy to the masses.

One of the key elements of Rockefeller's strategy was his ability to use Standard Oil stock as acquisition currency. He could buy up rival refineries with his highly valued stock, and he encouraged new entrants to stay out of the business by keeping his transportation costs so low that no other firm could meet his prices and make a profit at the same time.

What does Standard Oil have to do with the Internet? Just as oil exploration had very low entry barriers, so does the Web. In segment after segment, the cost of entry is low. As a result, virtually every segment of the Web business has hundreds if not thousands of small players. And just as Rockefeller did with the oil industry, some of the leading Web players have analyzed the industry to find its choke points, adapting their business strategies so that they can control the key choke points in the Web business.

Just as Rockefeller did with Standard Oil, the companies who are making money on the Web are the ones who have shaped their strategies to take advantage of the most powerful economic levers in their industries. Cisco Systems dominates network equipment because its control of the architecture at the brains of a corporate network forces all other equipment to work with the Cisco router. Kleiner Perkins dominates Internet venture capital because it has the best relations with technology sources, top-performing management teams, and first-class stock underwriters. And AOL Time Warner dominates the ISP business because it has attracted the highest number of eyeballs through its Web content and promotional skills. As a result, advertisers are willing to pay the most money to get access to the largest audience. These are the kinds of businesses that are making money on the Web.

For those who are exposed to the torrents of hype, it is hard not to conclude that the Internet will change everything. The foregoing comparison of the Internet and the oil industry is intended to persuade you that, while the content of the Internet business is somewhat unique, its form follows historical patterns that are not without precedent. *E-Leaders* uses the methods of industrial organization economics to analyze specific Internet business segments. The result is a map that will help investors and managers chart a profitable course through the apparent chaos that is today's world of Internet business.

02

Definition of Terms

E-leaders have introduced new management processes, the understanding of which demands an understanding of new management concepts. This chapter defines the following elements of the new management vocabulary, including:

» the Net Profit Retriever;
» the Web Business Pyramid; and
» the Web Applications Pyramid.

To analyze Internet business, various terms will be used which will now be defined.

Following are three practical frameworks with which we will make business sense of the Internet. The first is aimed mainly at the investor, the second at Internet business managers, the third at non-Internet business managers. But no matter what hat you are wearing, you will probably find that all three frameworks enlarge your Internet business understanding. Even if you are simply someone who wants to understand the Internet as an important new aspect of global culture, you will benefit from understanding these frameworks. I call them:

» Net Profit Retriever
» Web Business Pyramid
» Web Applications Pyramid.

FOR INVESTORS: THE NET PROFIT RETRIEVER

They say that if you want a friend on Wall Street, get a dog. Many Wall Street tycoons own golden retrievers. To invest in Internet companies, we need a Net Profit Retriever.

The Net Profit Retriever can put its nose to the ground and sniff out net profits.

The Net Profit Retriever works like a finely tuned investment filter. Put any Internet company in front of it, and the Net Profit Retriever will tell you whether the company is likely to be a good long-term investment.

The Net Profit Retriever has a particularly sensitive nose for sniffing out good Internet companies. Instead of the normal number of nostrils, it has three. One nostril sniffs for the industry, the second for the company's strategy, and the third for its management. If the scents of all three are right, the Net Profit Retriever barks three times to tell you that the company is a worthy investment.

What exactly does it take to get the Net Profit Retriever to bark three times? First, the Internet company must be competing in an industry with economic leverage. Economic leverage means that the companies in the industry sell a product that is so important to its customers and in such scarce supply that these companies can charge a very high price. If an industry comprising ten companies controlled all the world's water supply, that industry would have virtually unlimited economic leverage.

Second, the company should offer its customers a closed-loop solution. A closed-loop solution means that the company provides all the services a customer needs to get the economic benefit for which the customer bought the product or service in the first place. In our fictional water industry, the company that finds the source, purifies the water, pipes it to your home, pulls the glass from the cabinet, drops in the ice cubes, fills it with water, and serves it to you with dinner is offering a closed-loop solution.

Third, the company's management must be able to adapt effectively to rapid change. This ability is particularly important because Internet time is said to be measured in dog years. (Good thing we have a Net Profit Retriever.) If people suddenly decided to change their drinking habits from all water to all milk, the company with the most agile management would be the first in the water industry to plug a limitless supply of milk into its distribution channel.

The Net Profit Retriever is a framework that investors can use to help evaluate Internet businesses. It does not attempt to develop definitive assessments of the dollar value of an Internet business, because as we will see, such valuation is often nearly impossible. But it does provide a way to see where profits are most likely. As we will also see, the stock market tends to reward companies that are the leaders in the most attractive Internet business segments.

FOR INTERNET BUSINESS MANAGERS: THE WEB BUSINESS PYRAMID

For Internet business managers, the most striking characteristic of Web businesses is the rapid pace of change. Internet business managers need a framework that can help them think about where their company should head and how it should get there. Investors should take note also, so that they understand where their investments are headed.

The pyramid shape implies a process of aspiration and attrition. Most Web businesses start out at the bottom of the pyramid. Few survivors make it to the top.

Level I: Lossware

Lossware refers to Web businesses that are destined to lose money. At this level, barriers to entry are very low; that is, it is easy for new firms to enter the market. Customers have no switching costs, meaning that it is easy for them to take their business elsewhere. Vendors spend virtually all their money in what seems like an unending loop of marketing and other expenses. The result of the spending is most often competitive parity, not competitive advantage. Many firms, and in fact there may even be some whole segments of the industry, do not survive this level.

One such industry segment, which we will explore in Chapter Ten, is the Web browser business. Web browsers let people navigate the Internet. In the early 1990s, browser technology was widely available and to create new browsers required only a few programmers. Netscape was the first to achieve dramatic commercial success with the browser; however, there were few barriers to entry. Microsoft built a competing product and gave it away for free. The Web browser business effectively ceased to exist. Its entire cost of development and marketing became a marketing giveaway, and nothing remained that could be used to earn revenues.

Level II: Brandware

Brandware is a group of businesses that have the potential to be profitable if the most heavily promoted brand survives and the weaker ones fold. In Brandware businesses, the industry is still highly fragmented, implying that the cost of entry is quite low. However, in this sector it is becoming clear that customers are really not interested in sifting through the offerings of seventy different vendors, tending to buy from whoever has the most compelling marketing message. Customers also want to buy from a vendor likely to survive the inevitable industry consolidation. Inherent in this level of the pyramid is the notion of a shakeout. By definition, fewer vendors will survive to climb to the top level of the pyramid.

Web portals exemplify Brandware business (Yahoo is a familiar example). This industry segment started off as a few companies trying to simplify the Web's massive complexity by providing users with a site that would help them search the Web for various content. Web portal firms started generally as search engines, and as in the Web browser business, they gave away the service for free. In short, Web portals started off as Lossware.

Web portals evolved into Brandware because it became clear that there was the potential to get companies to advertise on them. Managers of the search engine companies recognized that the value of their business increased in relation to the number of visitors to their Website. So, these companies began trying to create switching costs between themselves, advertisers, and site visitors. These efforts, including chat sites, personalization, news, shopping, and a host of other services, were intended to get visitors to spend enough time at the sites to make them attractive targets for advertisers. Thus arose the idea that Web portals are brandable.

However, Web portals are expensive to maintain. Fierce competition for visitors and advertising has forced a few of the smaller players to sell out to media companies with deep pockets. It is possible that a small number of large Web portals will survive, and because these survivors may "control" access to large numbers of visitors whose tastes and interests are well understood, they may be able to achieve economic leverage over advertisers.

Level III: Powerware

Powerware refers to businesses that generate consistently high returns. Powerware businesses enjoy economic leverage and offer customers closed-loop solutions. The economic leverage comes from offering a valuable product or service that is in scarce supply because most competitors have been squeezed out; and the closed-loop solution is delivered to raise the switching costs between vendors and customers to such a high level that new entrants are effectively locked out.

In some cases, Brandware evolved into Powerware, as has occurred in the venture capital industry, which originally consisted of a fairly small number of firms. The ones that made winning investments tended to emerge as survivors when pension funds and endowments came along to make the next round of investments.

Internet venture capital firms help build Internet companies by providing capital, hiring management teams, and gaining access to the public equity markets. They have used their own willingness to risk capital in start-up companies and the cyclical nature of capital markets as levers to grab control over two additional elements of economic value creation: management talent and access to premier underwriters. As a result of this control, leading venture firms have powerful economic leverage.

FOR NON-INTERNET BUSINESS MANAGERS: THE WEB APPLICATIONS PYRAMID

For non-Internet business managers, the most important challenge is to understand the incremental costs and benefits of moving their business to the Web. Non-Internet business managers need a framework that can help them evaluate these costs and benefits depending on their company's current level of "Webification" and its business objectives. The Web Applications Pyramid is such a framework.

Many companies are in the Level I, online brochure stage, putting product literature, annual reports, and other information traditionally in print form on their Website.

Some companies have begun to use the Web as a means of collecting order forms. The order information gathered via the Web is then printed out and used as an input into an unchanged order fulfillment process. Because these companies do not integrate the ordering information into their back-end processes, they are at Level II, front-end transaction applications.

Whereas many companies have implemented applications near the base of the pyramid, very few companies have built the kinds of application that are at the top. It is rare for a firm to start with Level III. More often, firms work their way up through the levels. They learn important corporate lessons at each level enabling them to perform more effectively when they move up.

A few companies, such as Dell and Cisco, have installed integrated transaction applications that tap into the full power of the Web, such as using the Web to exchange information with customers; such information being tightly linked with the internal operations of the company. These applications are referred to as Level III, integrated applications.

NINE INTERNET BUSINESS SEGMENTS

An Internet business is a company that derives some or all of its revenues through the Internet. From my research, I have concluded that there are nine Internet business segments, each of which is a distinct industry with unique competitors, customers, profit dynamics, and requirements for competitive success. The nine Internet business segments are:

1 Network infrastructure
2 Web consulting
3 Internet venture capital
4 Internet security
5 Web portals
6 Electronic commerce
7 Web content
8 Internet service providers
9 Web commerce tools.

Let's define each of these Internet business segments in turn.

Network infrastructure

Network infrastructure is the hardware that directs traffic over the Internet. It consists mainly of devices called routers, switches, hubs, bridges, and network interface cards. Vendors of this equipment include Cisco Systems, 3Com, Cabletron, Juniper Networks, Lucent, and Nortel Networks.

Web consulting

Web consulting firms help organizations use the Web to improve their competitive positions. They accomplish this, first, by working with client executives to understand their business objectives. Then the Web consultants design and implement Web-based systems that help the clients achieve their objectives. Web consultants include Sapient, Proxicom, and DiamondCluster International.

Internet venture capital

Internet venture capital firms provide capital, recruit managers, and help grow Internet companies so that they can go public and generate high investment returns. This sector includes Kleiner Perkins, Integral Capital Partners, Institutional Venture Partners, Internet Capital Group, and CMGI.

Internet security

Internet security firms provide software and services that help protect organizations' information networks from unauthorized intrusion and tampering. They accomplish this by providing such services as ethical hacking, in which an authorized individual attempts to break into a firm's information network to identify security weaknesses. Internet security firms also sell a variety of software products that are designed to plug such weaknesses. These security firms include CheckPoint Software Technologies, Network Associates, and RSA Security.

Web portals

Web portals give Internet visitors a place to begin their exploration of the Internet. They do this by offering search engines, e-mail, information services, chat, and other services. Some firms in this segment are attempting to make the Web their primary mode of transaction. Others are adding Web channels to existing conventional modes of business. Web portals seek to attract as many visitors as possible so that companies will view the Web portal as an attractive place to advertise. They include Yahoo, Excite@Home, and Terra Lycos.

Electronic commerce

Electronic commerce (e-commerce) is the selling of products and services using the Internet. E-commerce firms let people trade securities, buy books and CDs, purchase computer hardware and software, obtain air tickets, reserve hotels, conduct online auctions, and purchase many other products and services. They include E-Trade Group, Amazon.com, Travelocity, and eBay.

Web content

Web content firms produce news about and analysis of the Internet. They hire reporters and consultants who collect information about the Internet, and transmit the Internet related information and analysis through a variety of media, including magazines, newspapers, TV, radio, trade shows, and the Internet itself. Most Web content firms also produce content about other technologies besides the Web. These firms include CNET, Gartner Group, Ziff-Davis, and CMP Media.

Internet service providers

Internet service providers (ISPs) provide individuals and organizations with connections to the Internet, using a variety of media that includes telephone wires, cable TV, regular TV, and eventually low earth orbiting (LEO) satellite networks. ISPs include Earthlink, Microsoft Network, and Exodus Communications.

Web commerce tools

Web commerce tools help organizations conduct business over the Web. These tools include advertising management services and software, Web browsers, multimedia broadcast tools, search engines, and online catalogue software. Web commerce tool vendors include Ariba, DoubleClick, NetGravity, Netscape, Macromedia, Inktomi, Commerce One, and Open Market.

03

Evolution

The Internet began with a US Department of Defense project to build a computer network that would be able to withstand a nuclear attack. This chapter traces the Internet's development, including:

» an essay on the evolution of the Internet since the 1960s; and
» a timeline that traces key events in the Internet's evolution.

THE PHENOMENAL FOUNDATION OF E-COMMERCE

The Internet was the result of some visionary thinking by certain people in the early 1960s who saw great potential value in allowing computers to share information on research and development in scientific and military fields. J.C.R. Licklider of the Massachusetts Institute of Technology (MIT) first proposed a global network of computers in 1962, and moved over to the Defense Advanced Research Projects Agency (DARPA) in late 1962 to head the work to develop it. Leonard Kleinrock of MIT and later University of California, Los Angeles (UCLA) developed the theory of packet switching, which was to form the basis of Internet connections. Lawrence Roberts of MIT connected a Massachusetts computer with a California computer in 1965 over dial-up telephone lines. It showed the feasibility of wide area networking, but also showed that the telephone line's circuit switching was inadequate. Kleinrock's packet switching theory was confirmed. Roberts moved over to DARPA in 1966 and developed his plan for ARPANET.

The Internet, then known as ARPANET, was brought online in 1969 under a contract led by the renamed Advanced Research Projects Agency (ARPA), and initially connected four major computers at universities in the south-western US (UCLA, Stanford Research Institute, University of California, Santa Barbara [UCSB], and the University of Utah). The contract was carried out by Bolt, Beranek, and Newman (BBN) of Cambridge, MA, under Bob Kahn and went online in December 1969. By June 1970, MIT, Harvard, BBN, and Systems Development Corporation (SDC) in Santa Monica, CA, were added. By January 1971, Stanford University, MIT's Lincoln Labs, Carnegie-Mellon, and Case Western Reserve University were added. In months to come, NASA/Ames, Mitre, Burroughs, Rand Corporation, and the University of Illinois plugged in. After that, there were far too many to keep listing here.

The Internet was designed in part to provide a communications network that would work even if some of the sites were destroyed by nuclear attack. If the most direct route was not available, the system would direct traffic around the network via alternative routes. The early Internet was used by computer experts, engineers, scientists, and librarians. There was nothing friendly about it, there being no home or office personal computers in those days, and anyone who used it, whether a computer professional or an engineer or scientist or librarian, had to learn to use a very complex system.

E-mail was adapted for ARPANET by Ray Tomlinson of BBN in 1972. He picked the @ symbol from the available symbols on his teletype to link the username and address. The telnet protocol, enabling logging on to a remote computer, was published as a Request for Comments (RFC) in 1972. RFCs are a means of sharing developmental work throughout the development community.

Libraries began automating and networking their catalogs in the late 1960s independently of ARPA. The visionary Frederick G. Kilgour of the Ohio College Library Center led networking of Ohio libraries during the 1960s and 1970s. In the mid-1970s more regional consortia from New England, the Southwest states, and the Middle Atlantic states, and others, joined with Ohio to form a national, later international, network.

The Internet matured in the 1970s as a result of the architecture first proposed by Bob Kahn at BBN and further developed by Kahn and Vint Cerf at Stanford, and others, throughout the 70s. It was adopted by the Defense Department in 1980 replacing the earlier Network Control Protocol (NCP) and universally adopted by 1983. In 1986, the National Science Foundation funded NSFNet as a cross-country 56 kbps backbone for the Internet. They maintained their sponsorship for nearly a decade, setting rules for its non-commercial government and research uses.

As the commands for using the Internet were standardized, it became easier for non-technical people to learn to use the networks. It was not easy by today's standards by any means, but it did open up use of the Internet to many more people, in universities in particular. Other departments besides the libraries, computer, physics, and engineering departments found ways to make good use of the networks – to communicate with colleagues around the world and to share files and resources.

In 1991, the first really friendly interface to the Internet was developed at the University of Minnesota. The University wanted to develop a simple menu system to access files and information on campus through their local network. A debate followed between mainframe adherents and those who believed in smaller systems. The mainframe adherents won the debate initially, but since the client–server advocates said they could put up a prototype very quickly, they were given the go-ahead to do a demonstration system. The resulting system was called a "gopher" after the University's mascot – the golden gopher. It proved to be very prolific, and within a few years there were over 10,000 gophers around the world. In a gopher system, you type or click on a number to select the menu selection you want.

In 1989 another significant event took place in making the nets easier to use. Tim Berners-Lee and others at the European Laboratory for Particle Physics, more popularly known as CERN, proposed a new protocol for information distribution. This protocol, which became the World Wide Web in 1991, was based on hypertext – a system of embedding links in text to link to other text, which you have been using every time you selected a text link if reading these pages online. Although started before gopher, it was slower to develop.

The development in 1993 of the graphical browser Mosaic by Marc Andreesen and his team at the University of Illinois gave the protocol its big boost. Later, Andreesen moved to become the brains behind Netscape, which produced the most successful graphical type of browser and server until Microsoft declared war and developed its Microsoft Internet Explorer.

Since the Internet was initially funded by the government, it was originally limited to research, education, and government uses. Commercial uses were prohibited unless they directly served the goals of research and education. This policy continued until the early 90s, when independent commercial networks began to grow. It then became possible to route traffic across the country from one commercial site to another without passing through the government-funded NSFNet Internet backbone.

Delphi was the first national commercial online service to offer Internet access to its subscribers. It opened up an e-mail connection in July 1992 and full Internet service in November 1992. All pretenses of limitations on commercial use disappeared in May 1995 when the National Science Foundation ended its sponsorship of the Internet backbone, and all traffic relied on commercial networks. AOL, Prodigy, and CompuServe came online. Since commercial usage was now so widespread, and educational institutions had been paying their own way for some time, the loss of NSF funding had no appreciable effect on costs.

INTERNET TIMELINE

1962 The RAND Corporation begins research into robust, distributed communication networks for military command and control.

1962–1969 The Internet is first conceived in the early 1960s. Under the leadership of the Department of Defense's (DOD) Advanced Research Project Agency (ARPA), it grows from a paper architecture into a small network (ARPANET) intended to promote the sharing of super-computers amongst researchers in the United States.

1965 DOD's Advanced Research Project Association begins work on ARPANET.

1965 ARPA sponsors research into a "co-operative network of time-sharing computers."

1967 First ARPANET papers presented at Association for Computing Machinery Symposium.

1967 Delegates at a symposium for the Association for Computing Machinery in Gatlingberg, TN, discuss the first plans for the ARPANET.

1968 First generation of networking hardware and software designed.

1969 ARPANET connects first four universities in the United States. Researchers at four US campuses create the first hosts of the ARPANET, connecting Stanford Research Institute, UCLA, UCSB, and the University of Utah.

1970 ALOHANET developed at the University of Hawaii.

1970–1973 The ARPANET is a success from the very beginning. Although originally designed to allow scientists to share data and access remote computers, e-mail quickly becomes the most popular application. ARPANET becomes a high-speed digital post office as people use it to collaborate on research projects and discuss topics of various interests.

1971 ARPANET grows to 23 hosts connecting universities and government research centers around the country.

1972 The InterNetworking Working Group becomes the first of several standards-setting entities to govern the growing network.

Vinton Cerf is elected the first chairman of the INWG, and later becomes known as a "Father of the Internet."

1973 ARPANET goes international with connections to University College in London, England and the Royal Radar Establishment in Norway.

1974 BBN opens Telnet, the first commercial version of the ARPANET.

1974–1981 The general public gets its first vague hint of how networked computers can be used in daily life as the commercial version of the ARPANET goes online. The ARPANET starts to move away from its military/research roots.

1975 Internet operations transferred to the Defense Communications Agency.

1976 Queen Elizabeth goes online with the first royal e-mail message.

1977 Unix-to-Unix Copy Program (UUCP) provides e-mail on THEORYNET.

1978 Transmission Control Protocol (TCP) checksum design finalized.

1979 Tom Truscott and Jim Ellis, two graduate students at Duke University, and Steve Bellovin at the University of North Carolina establish the first USENET newsgroups. Users from all over the world join these discussion groups to talk about the Net, politics, religion, and thousands of other subjects.

1981 ARPANET has 213 hosts. A new host is added approximately once every 20 days.

1982 The term "Internet" is used for the first time.

1982–1987 Bob Kahn and Vint Cerf are key members of a team which creates TCP/IP (Internet Protocol), the common language of all Internet computers. For the first time the loose collection of networks which made up the ARPANET is seen as an "internet," and the Internet as we know it today is born.

The mid-80s marks a boom in the personal computer and super-minicomputer industries. The combination of inexpensive desktop machines and powerful, network-ready servers allows many companies to join the Internet for the first time. Corporations begin to use the Internet to communicate with each other and with their customers.

1983 TCP/IP becomes the universal language of the Internet.

1984 William Gibson coins the term "cyberspace" in his novel *Neuromancer*. The number of Internet hosts exceeds 1000.

1985 Internet e-mail and newsgroups now part of life at many universities.

1986 Case Western Reserve University in Cleveland, Ohio, creates the first "Freenet" for the Society for Public Access Computing.

1987 The number of Internet hosts exceeds 10,000.

1988 Internet worm unleashed.

1988-1990 By 1988 the Internet is an essential tool for communications; however, it also begins to create concerns about privacy and security in the digital world. New words, such as "hacker," "cracker" and "electronic break-in," are created.

These new worries are dramatically demonstrated on November 1, 1988 when a malicious program called the "Internet Worm" temporarily disables approximately 6000 of the 60,000 Internet hosts.

1988 The Computer Emergency Response Team (CERT) is formed to address security concerns raised by the Worm.

1989 System administrator turned author, Clifford Stoll, catches a group of "cyberspies," and writes the best-seller *The Cuckoo's Egg*. The number of Internet hosts exceeds 100,000.

1990 A happy victim of its own unplanned, unexpected success, the ARPANET is decommissioned, leaving only the vast network-of-networks called the Internet. The number of hosts exceeds 300,000.

1991 The World Wide Web is born!

1991-1993 Corporations wishing to use the Internet face a serious problem: commercial network traffic is banned from the National Science Foundation's NSFNET, the backbone of the Internet. In 1991 the NSF lifts the restriction on commercial use, clearing the way for the age of electronic commerce.

At the University of Minnesota, a team led by computer programmer Mark MaCahill releases "gopher," the first point-and-click way of navigating the files of the Internet in 1991. Originally designed to ease campus communications, gopher is freely distributed on the Internet. MaCahill calls it "the first Internet application my mom can use." 1991 is also the year in which Tim Berners-Lee, working at CERN in Switzerland, posts the first computer code of the World Wide Web in a relatively innocuous newsgroup, "alt.hypertext." The ability to combine words, pictures, and sounds on Web pages excites many computer programmers who see the potential for publishing information on the Internet in a way that can be as easy as using a word processor.

Marc Andreesen and a group of student programmers at NCSA (the National Center for Supercomputing Applications located on the campus of University of Illinois at Urbana Champaign) will eventually develop a graphical browser for the World Wide Web called Mosaic.

1991 Traffic on the NSF backbone network exceeds 1 trillion bytes per month.

1992 One million hosts have multimedia access to the Internet over the "Mbone."

1992 The first audio and video broadcasts take place over the portion of the Internet known as the Mbone. More than 1,000,000 hosts are part of the Internet.

1993 Mosaic, the first graphics-based Web browser, becomes available. Traffic on the Internet expands at a 341,634% annual growth rate.

1994 The Rolling Stones broadcast the Voodoo Lounge tour over the Mbone. Marc Andreesen and Jim Clark form Netscape Communications Corporation. Pizza Hut accepts orders for a mushroom, pepperoni with extra cheese over the Net, and Japan's prime minister goes online at www.kantei.go.jp. Backbone traffic exceeds 10 trillion bytes per month.

1995 NSFNET reverts back to a research project, leaving the Internet in commercial hands. The Web now comprises the bulk of Internet traffic. The Vatican launches www.vatican.va. James

Gosling and a team of programmers at Sun Microsystems release an Internet programming language called Java, which radically alters the way applications and information can be retrieved, displayed, and used over the Internet.

1996 Nearly 10 million hosts online. The Internet covers the globe.

1996 As the Internet celebrates its 25th anniversary, the military strategies that influenced its birth become historical footnotes. Approximately 40 million people are connected to the Internet. More than $1bn per year changes hands at Internet shopping malls, and Internet-related companies like Netscape are the darlings of high-tech investors.

Users in almost 150 countries around the world are now connected to the Internet. The number of computer hosts approaches 10 million.

Within 30 years, the Internet has grown from a Cold War concept for controlling the tattered remains of a post-nuclear society to the Information Superhighway. Just as the railroads of the nineteenth century enabled the machine age, and revolutionized the society of the time, the Internet takes us into the information age, and profoundly affects the world in which we live.

1998 Web size estimates range between 275 (Digital) and 320 (NEC) million pages for 1Q. Companies flock to the Turkmenistan NIC in order to register their name under the .tm domain, the English abbreviation for trademark.

1999 business.com is sold for $7.5mn – it was purchased in 1997 for $150,000 (November 30).

2000 The US timekeeper and a few other time services around the world report the New Year as 19100 on 1 Jan. A massive denial of service attack is launched against major Websites, including Yahoo, Amazon, and eBay in early February. Websize estimates by NEC-RI and Inktomi surpass 1 billion indexable pages.

2001 VeriSign extends its multilingual domain testbed to encompass various European languages (February 26), and later the full Unicode character set (April 5), opening up most of the world's languages.

04

The E-Dimension

Winning companies have found ways to profit from the use of the Internet in their business. This chapter shows how e-leaders use e-commerce to best advantage. It includes:

» Web myths and realities; and
» best practices in the use of the Internet for business.

This chapter is intended for managers whose firm currently may have nothing to do with the Web or is beginning to use the Web as a new channel for conducting its business. The Web can help organizations become more profitable. However, managers will not be able to harness its power until they change their way of thinking about it. In order to put managers into the right mindset, this chapter addresses several questions.

» What are the most commonly held myths about the Web and what are the realities?
» What can managers learn from examples of successful and less successful organizational efforts to use the Web?
» How can managers evaluate whether it makes sense for their companies to use the Web?
» For companies that do have the potential to benefit from the Web, what should managers do?
» What kinds of challenges should managers expect if they decide to use the Web and how can these challenges be addressed and overcome?

WEB MYTHS AND REALITIES

The air is filled with myths about the power of the Web to transform everything fundamentally. They have helped enrich a handful of venture capitalists and managers. However, large organizations and consumers are the intended audience for these myths, and in order not to become a victim a manager must parse them carefully. While managerial willingness to jump on the Internet bandwagon has helped investors and managers in the companies that sell Web products and services, the same benefits have not always flowed to the organizations that have tried to use the Web.

Myth: the Web will transform everything

In the view of John Doerr of Kleiner Perkins, if anything the Web is under-hyped. Doerr has tremendous resources at his disposal for promulgating this message. He had the ear of former Vice President Al Gore. He has influence in the high-tech and general business press

THE E-DIMENSION **27**

and many important Web news outlets. And he uses his access to these channels to communicate a message over and over in the media that helps increase the value of his investments.

Reality: the Web is a technology that can help organizations become more effective if it is used appropriately

As we have seen, the Web has created profit opportunities for some industries and some companies. If managers can find a way to use the Web to give them economic leverage within their system of value creation, then the Web can help enhance profits.

One example of this is General Electric (GE). GE and Thomson Publishing created a joint venture called Trade Processing Network (TPN). TPN helps companies use the Web to streamline corporate procurement of items such as office supplies. By increasing the percentage of corporate employees that buy office supplies through preferred suppliers, TPN can help a company reduce the unit costs of these supplies by up to 20%. For a large firm like GE with $5bn in annual office supply purchases, a 20% cost reduction translates into $1bn in annual savings.

But the TPN example is the exception that proves the rule. More frequently, managers get carried away by the superficial appeal of the technology. As a result, they often end up merely paving over the cow paths of their business with Web technology. Using this approach, it is easy for them to throw away $20mn on a systems project that delivers no payoff.

Myth: organizations that do not use the Web will soon perish

This line of reasoning is a corollary to the basic message that the Web will transform everything. Sales people often try to motivate managers by exhorting them not to be left behind. This message is directed most strongly at firms that are intermediaries. The reasoning goes that the middlemen will be squeezed out as the Web bypasses their role in the economic system.

Reality: in many industries, the Web is unlikely to create much advantage

Often, e-commerce startups are trying to use the Web to bypass intermediaries. However, many of these startups are losing huge amounts of money, and the incumbent intermediaries are not losing significant market share. Because the incumbents have greater financial resources, they may ultimately find themselves in a position to acquire the stumbling startups. And through these acquisitions, they may be able to add a complementary distribution channel that makes life a bit easier for their customers.

Myth: e-commerce will become a huge factor in the world economy

Countless pundits forecast trillions of e-commerce revenues by the year 2002. These projections do play an important role in raising capital for firms that have the phrase ".com" in their name. How these projections are derived and what assumptions they are based on remains a bit murky. Nevertheless, the motivation for the projections is clear.

Reality: e-commerce is likely to be a small part of the global economy at least through the year 2003

According to an October 1998 study by the Organization for Economic Co-operation and Development (OECD) in Paris, e-commerce, especially in the consumer market, would remain a small percentage of overall retail sales for at least the next five years and would not have a significant impact on the global economy anytime soon. Including the more lucrative business-to-business (b2b) e-commerce market, which the OECD predicted would account for about 80% of overall e-commerce through the next five years, global e-commerce revenues could reach $1trn by 2003 according to *The Industry Standard*. This figure is a mere 15% of the overall retail sales predicted for a selection of seven OECD member countries in 2003. And business-to-consumer (b2c) e-commerce should account for just 20% of the total revenues generated by e-commerce in 2003, or $200bn.

The OECD study says that the convenience and mass customization of b2c e-commerce are advantages, but adds that their success is not assured. The report suggests that b2c e-commerce may become merely another channel for retailers, such as mail order, rather than a new dominant mode of commerce. The report also notes that 80% of online commerce today is conducted in the US, and that visions of global e-commerce must be tempered by the reality that half of the world's population has never made a telephone call, much less accessed the Internet.

Myth: the Web is the single greatest source of legal wealth creation in human history

Venture capitalist John Doerr discusses the billions of market capitalization and hundreds of thousands of jobs created by Web companies. While it is not clear how the figures he cites were generated, it is not difficult to concede that the levels of stockholder value and employment are tremendous. The question is, how has the wealth been created and distributed? And how real is it?

Reality: the Web has enriched a very small number of investors and managers and has yet to realize its promise in terms of enriching organizations

Venture firms are arbitrageurs. They purchase ownership of technology startups in one market where they are cheap and resell their stakes in another market where they are dear. When a startup is about to close down because it has run out of cash, a venture capitalist can purchase a big chunk of the company for relatively little money. And when the market for initial public offerings is strong, that same venture capitalist can turn around and sell the bargain-priced equity at 10 to 20 times the purchase price. This is perfectly legal.

One of the reasons that venture capitalists can sell their shares in the public market is that they are able to include the names of large, prestigious organizations on their customer list. But unless the Web can create tangible value for these organizations, they will ultimately be mere pawns in the venture capitalists' arbitrage play.

Since April 2000, $5trn in stock market wealth has been lost as a consequence of the bubble economy that Doerr helped to spur. In fact, as of July 2001, Doerr has announced an effort to backpedal from his statement, so perhaps he can salvage his reputation in the eyes of some naïve economic historian.

LESSONS FROM EXPERIENCE WITH THE WEB

Some organizations such as Cisco and Dell have profited from their use of the Web. Many of these organizations have achieved qualitative improvements in their operations, including the ability to solve customer service problems faster, or a reduction in the level of rework in order processing. It makes intuitive sense that if customers place billions of dollars worth of orders via the Web, the sales staff can be freed up to spend more time trying to close deals with new customers. And while Cisco describes savings in the hundreds of millions, most of the savings come from the ability to run a larger operation without needing to hire as many people. So the cost savings are quantified by comparing actual staff levels to a forecast of the number of staff that would have been on Cisco's payroll if the system were not in place.

These success stories highlight an important point about the organizational benefits of using the Web. The Web can increase the efficiency and effectiveness of repetitive operational processes. It can help organizations set up processes that reduce errors in configuring orders even as these processes handle high transaction volumes. For example, Cisco's Cisco Connection Online Website (CCO) helps customers to configure their orders for new network equipment so that the product meets their needs and can be manufactured.

While firms have used other means of performing electronic processing, such as Electronic Data Interchange (EDI), the Web is less expensive. EDI is a standard format for transmitting electronic documents such as purchase orders and invoices. It is very costly for companies with many suppliers to set up a system using EDI because they must change their systems and those of their suppliers to make all trading partners adhere to the EDI standards. Once firms have made the investment, however, they are reluctant to throw it out for the next new technology.

Nevertheless, a study by International Data Corporation indicates that 80% of the companies that use EDI are expected to shift 30% of their traffic over to the Web by 2003. The reason is that the Web is a cheaper way to transmit information. With the hybrid of EDI and Web technology, these companies will be able to enjoy the cost advantages of the Web without overhauling the systems that are programmed for EDI.

The Web can also tap into a common experience base that helps to solve problems more quickly. For example, Cisco's CCO Website lets customers tap into the cumulative experience of Cisco's global customer base. As a result, a customer service person in California will have access to the solution to an obscure technical problem that was solved by a service technician in Australia. Without access to that global experience base, the customer might have spent weeks reinventing a solution.

BEST PRACTICES

Here are eight best practices that managers should consider based on the experience of organizations that have used the Web.

1 *The CEO needs to be a Web user.* If CEOs do not have personal experience with the Web, it is difficult for them to understand how the technology can help the business. The CEO needs to experience the power of the Web for tasks such as sending e-mail to friends and family, checking their stock portfolio, or getting information about a hobby. Once they have a feeling for what the Web can do at a personal level, they will begin to imagine how it can help improve the business.

2 *The Web-based solution must be driven by competitive strategy.* Managers must understand how the Web relates to competitive strategy. Making this connection is difficult in the absence of a commonly understood methodology for doing so, a deficiency we will address below. With effective strategy, Internet profiteers used the Web to help them increase revenues as much as 70% a year while adding even more to their bottom lines. The source of these incremental profits is better customer service with the same number of employees.

3 *There should be a partnership between IS and the business.* Unfortunately, many organizations have a long history of emotional volatility in the relationship between information

services (IS) and business managers. The IS managers promise the business managers great results from a new technology but are unable to deliver. Dialogue lapses into blame and punishment.

In the organizations that have earned Internet profits, the situation is different. In these organizations, there is a true partnership between IS and business management. Business managers bring up practical problems and IS propose solutions. As the solution evolves, business and IS work together because the success of the enterprise depends on their teamwork. Since the solution is linked to the success of the business (and of the stock options of both sets of management), both parties have a strong incentive to work together to overcome obstacles.

4 *Management has to set measurable objectives for the system.* A truism of management is that what gets measured, gets done. Conversely, what does not get measured does not get done. Different groups within an organization value different things, which leads to different performance measures. For example, IS may tend to measure itself in terms of how many people are working on cutting-edge technologies. But executive management is likely to measure itself on earnings growth and stock price performance. In order to make an electronic commerce initiative work, management must set the objectives in a way that is meaningful for the business and IS.

In short, management should define the problem in terms that matter to the entire organization, not just one part. The goal might be to have 50% of sales coming from the Web within two years, or to increase revenues 50% a year while keeping customer service headcount constant. Whatever the goal, it is important that it be specific, measurable and understandable by all members of the team that is charged with achieving it.

5 *Management should direct the efforts of a cross-functional team to change the business process.* It is increasingly clear that using the Web to enhance corporate competitiveness is not something that the CEO can delegate to middle management. The reason that the CEO must lead the process is that the Web

can only be a tool for enhancing competitiveness if the different functions within the company work together to create more value for customers. Unless the CEO creates strong incentives for such teamwork, the Web technology will not be a useful competitive tool.

6 *The back-end operations and systems must work together with the Web front-end.* Consistent with the theme of teamwork among people is the need for teamwork among systems. The Web can make it very easy for a customer to place an order. This friendly front-end creates an implicit promise that the order fulfillment process will be equally satisfying to the customer. If a company's fulfillment processes are inefficient and complex, then the customer's expectations for service will be raised but ultimately disappointed. If a firm is going to invest in making its front-end operations very easy to use without simultaneously improving the back-end systems, then the firm might be better off not using the Web at all.

Dell has figured this out. Before it developed its Website, Dell had developed an order fulfillment process that worked effectively. The company created a "built-to-order" process for manufacturing and delivering computers. Its manufacturing and delivery process produced benefits for shareholders and customers. Dell shareholders were rewarded with higher profit growth because the company did not incur the costs of carrying excess inventory. Customers were better off because they were able to purchase a computer that was configured specifically to meet their needs. And when they placed an order, it was delivered promptly and predictably.

When Dell decided to build its Website, its order fulfillment processes were already quite effective. The Website made it possible for people to buy computers configured in a standard fashion at their desired price level. People could place their order over the Web and Dell would take the order and fulfill it just as quickly and effectively as it had in the past. As of October 1988, Dell's success was evidenced by its $5mn a day worth of computer sales.

7 *In many cases, the Web is a parallel channel for exchanging information and distributing product.*. Adding a parallel channel can be perceived as a threat to the hegemony of the existing channels. If a company has a direct sales force and a telephone sales force, both will feel threatened by the addition of the Web distribution channel. The fear is that the Web will siphon away sales that might have been made by the direct and telephone sales forces. And since the Web does not need to get sales commissions, the competing channels may see the Web as a threat to their long-term survival. There are no easy solutions to this problem. However, if the CEO leads the cross-functional team, there will be a forum for addressing it.

Office Depot's recent addition of a Web-based distribution channel is a case in point. Office Depot worked closely with its customers to design a Website that would be easy to use. Since the company already sold office supplies through both direct and telephone sales, the Web-based channel represented a potential threat. However, management made it clear to the incumbent sales channels that the firm needed to add a Web-channel to sustain Office Depot's competitiveness. The result is that the incumbent channels will need to develop new strategies to maintain their revenue growth.

8 *Despite these lessons, each company must experiment and learn how to use the Web itself.* There is very little established dogma about how best to use the Web to enhance a company's performance. This lack of experience is keeping many companies from using the Web. More adventurous companies have realized that this lack of certainty is a psychological barrier to entry for competitors. So the adventurous companies get started. They identify pieces of a solution that can be implemented and evaluated quickly. They do more of what succeeds and learn from what fails. Regardless of the outcome, they keep trying until they have achieved significant success. And this success emboldens them to try more.

05

The Global Dimension

Globalization and the Internet have evolved together over the last several years. This chapter highlights this co-evolution, providing a roadmap for managers. It includes:

» an essay on the emergence of globalization and the Internet;
» key issues for management of globalization and technology; and
» best practices for harnessing globalization and the Internet to strengthen a firm's competitive position.

The Internet provides tools for organizations seeking to globalize. In order to capture the full value of the Internet, firms must understand how their global strategies position them for sustainable competitive advantage and how to employ the Internet as an enabler of that advantage.

The history of the Internet, from US defense network to international "virtual college" of scientific and academic researchers to globally expanding World Wide Web, has been one of exponential growth in both number of users and number of hosts connected to the network. While still heavily dominated by the United States in terms of numbers of both users and hosts, the Internet is now widely accessible in all industrialized countries and in major cities of most developing countries. Attempts to extend access within developing countries, however, have been slowed by telecommunications links that are unavailable, unreliable, and/or unaffordable. Now both the telecommunications industry, eager to expand into new markets, and policymakers, convinced that new communications technologies are critical to economic growth, are heeding the call to improve the global "information infrastructure."

This chapter examines issues surrounding access to the Internet in developing countries and the utilization of this powerful information tool for social and economic development. It begins with a discussion of the current national demographics of the Internet, and continues with a description of some of the key issues that these demographic differences raise for managers. The chapter concludes with a set of best practices for globalization and the Internet.

ACCESS TO THE INTERNET: GROWTH AND GAPS

Statistics on Internet access reveal the extent of the discrepancies between high- and low-income nations (see Table 5.1). In 1995, high-income countries had almost 25,000 Internet users per one million inhabitants, while lower-middle income countries had fewer than 1000. The poorest countries had fewer than 20 Internet users per one million inhabitants. The extreme scarcity of hosts (uniquely reachable connected computers) in poorer, developing countries indicates that access to the Internet there is both difficult and expensive.

Perhaps the most striking development for both industrialized and developing countries has been the recent exponential growth of the

Table 5.1 Internet access by country classification, 1995

Country classification	Internet users/mn people	Internet hosts/mn people
High income	24,679.5	10,749.2
Upper-middle income	3,757.5	380.1
Lower-middle income	811.6	73.3
Low income	17.4	1.4

Internet as measured by the number of hosts. Worldwide, the number of hosts grew from fewer than 100,000 in 1989 to more than 16 million by early 1997. Internet domains (site addresses, such as those ending in ".com," ".org," ".edu," or a two-digit country code) have also proliferated. The number of Internet domains grew exponentially, from 21,000 in December 1992 to 828,000 in December 1996; growth accelerated sharply in 1995 with increased access to the World Wide Web. And while the United States accounts for the vast majority of Internet sites, this exponential trend was mirrored by many other industrialized countries and also by lower-middle-income and some low-income countries, although the absolute number of sites connected varied from more than 120,000 in major industrialized countries to fewer than 1000 in some developing countries.

Growth in Internet access has been consistently strong, but it is important to analyze the potential for widespread access to determine whether these growth rates are likely to continue. Two important indicators of this potential are teledensity, the availability of infrastructure that connects users to the Internet (measured in telephone lines per 100 inhabitants), and computer density, the availability of computer equipment needed for Internet access (measured in computers per 100 inhabitants). (See Table 5.2.)

Industrialized countries possess, on average, more than 50 telephone lines and 20 computers per 100 people. (There is considerable range in computer access even in industrialized countries: while the United States has more than 30 computers per 100 people, Germany, France, and Japan have fewer than half that number.) Lower-middle-income countries and low-income countries lag far behind in access

Table 5.2   Teledensity and computer density, 1995.

Country classification	Telephone lines/100 people	PCs/100 people
High income	53.2	20.5
Upper-middle income	14.5	3.3
Lower-middle income	9.1	1.1
Low income	2.0	0.2

to both telecommunications and information technologies. Lower-middle-income countries have only about nine telephone lines and one computer per 100 inhabitants; the poorest countries have very limited access to telecommunications and only about one computer for every 500 people.

Major disparities also exist within the developing world. Industrializing Asian economies such as the Four Tigers (Hong Kong, South Korea, Singapore, and Taiwan) have invested much more in information and communication technologies than have Latin American countries and the emerging economies of Eastern Europe, and are generally outstripping them in access both to telecommunications and to computers. (See Table 5.3.)

As these statistics show, an enormous information gap still exists between industrialized and developing countries, and among developing countries themselves, in terms of access to both computers and the telecommunications infrastructure necessary to link them to the Internet.

MANAGERIAL ISSUES OF GLOBALIZATION AND THE INTERNET

For general managers, these demographic differences raise strategic issues such as the following examples.

» What opportunities and threats does globalization present to managers?
» Does the Internet protect against the threats of globalization or does it exacerbate them?
» Does the Internet hinder or help managers to take advantage of the opportunities created by globalization?

Table 5.3 Access in emerging economies, 1995.

Country	Telephone lines/100 people	PCs/100 people
Hong Kong	53.0	11.6
South Korea	41.5	12.1
Malaysia	16.6	4.0
Singapore	47.9	17.2
Taiwan	43.1	8.3
Czech Republic	23.7	5.3
Hungary	18.5	3.9
Poland	14.8	2.9
Ukraine	16.1	0.6
Argentina	16.0	2.5
Brazil	7.5	1.3
Chile	13.2	3.8
Mexico	9.6	2.6
Venezuela	11.1	1.7

» Should globalization be subsumed by the Internet in consideration of corporate strategy or should the Internet be the driving force?

» What is the best roadmap for integrating globalization with the Internet in formulating corporate strategy?

» How can the costs and benefits of these factors be measured?

BEST PRACTICES

Integration of globalization and the Internet can enhance the competitiveness of specific activities. Simply put, the most successful marriage of globalization and the Internet gives customers more value for their money. Here are ten best practices designed to help managers deliver on this principle.

1. Create a cross-functional team

Firms that achieve results are able to harness the efforts of different departments in order to develop and implement successful change. To globalize and use the Internet effectively, firms should create an internal team consisting of all parties that will be affected by the new process. Team participants may include senior management, information technology, finance, sales, purchasing, manufacturing, key suppliers, lead customers, and distributors.

2. Understand the customer

Since creating superior customer value is the principle that drives successful globalization enhanced by the Internet, the cross-functional team must research customers. This research may focus on a particular activity such as technical service or product development. Through the research, the cross-functional team should understand specific, ranked criteria for assessing the activity, how well the firm performs this activity, and where the customer believes this activity could improve.

3. Identify the critical activities required to meet customer needs better than the competition

The next step is for the firm to analyze the steps in its current process and use this analysis to pinpoint opportunities for enhancing the customers' perceived value by cutting out wasted activity, and by targeting the process to create more value for customers.

4. Assess how well these activities are being performed relative to competitors

Firms may then choose to conduct a similar analysis of how its leading competitors perform these activities in order to identify specific steps that competitors perform better than your firm – and to identify the extent to which their performance of activities globally and/or through the use of the Internet provides them with a competitive advantage, or puts your firm at a competitive disadvantage.

5. Benchmark global leaders in performing the activities

Firms may also identify world-class companies outside their industry that are widely perceived as leaders in these activities. Again, the intent of this analysis is to identify valuable insights that your firm can use to enhance the way it performs them.

6. Consider ways of improving the way your firm performs these activities through globalization and the Internet

Based on the research performed in steps two through five, the cross-functional team is now in a strong position to identify ways to improve critical business processes by changing the geographic location where specific activities are performed, and by using the Internet to help co-ordinate these dispersed activities.

7. Envision the enhanced process

Using the ideas developed in step six, the cross-functional team can develop a more formalized vision of the enhanced process. For example, it might be described in terms of a process flow chart and a specific description of where the process steps would be performed, and how the Internet might be used to enable the result.

8. Implement a prototype of the improved process

This step involves turning the ideas developed in step seven into a working prototype of the enhanced process. In order to achieve the prototype, it is important to pick an important part of the new process that is complex and yet that will not sink your business if there are problems.

9. Test and refine the prototype

The purpose of this step is to work out potential kinks in the enhanced process so that it can be rolled out throughout your organization. This process should be tested on internal rather than paying customers. The organization should critique the prototype ruthlessly and work to refine the prototype quickly so that it can be relatively kink-free to plan the roll-out.

10. Roll out the new process globally

To roll out the new process globally demands effective planning. This planning should schedule extensive training of IT staff, process participants, and users. The planning should also include upgrades to systems, hiring plans, changes to compensation and human resources practices – where appropriate – and development of customer feedback mechanisms to ensure that the enhanced process continues to adapt in the future.

The State of the Art

Although the bubble burst, the Internet continues to evolve, so what are today's hot issues? This chapter explores the following topics:

» six concepts to help managers profit from the Internet; and
» three key changes in the competitive and investment environment likely to shape the future evolution of the Internet.

To help senior executives deal with the challenges of e-commerce, this book presents five key concepts that are designed to answer the five most essential questions that the subject raises for senior executives. Table 6.1 outlines these questions and concepts.

Table 6.1   Key questions and concepts of e-commerce.

Strategic issues	Key concept
What are our intangible assets and how can e-commerce help unlock their value?	Strategic balance sheet analysis
What opportunities for market share gain does e-commerce create for us and how does e-commerce threaten our competitive position?	Competitive opportunity and threat assessment
What risks does e-commerce introduce into our firm and how can we address these risks?	E-commerce risk evaluation
How can e-commerce transform the stock market's assessment of our firm's value?	Enterprise value assessment
How can our management team prioritize potential e-commerce projects to guide the allocation of capital and people?	E-commerce portfolio analysis

STRATEGIC BALANCE SHEET ANALYSIS

With the advent of e-commerce, financial executives are finding that the return on capital is higher from investing in intangible assets than in tangible ones. As a result, financial executives need a way to pinpoint the intangible assets with the greatest potential to increase their firm's shareholder value. Strategic balance sheet analysis is such a process.

Strategic balance sheet analysis consists of three steps. First a firm must identify its intangible assets. Then the firm must conceptualize e-commerce applications that can extract value from these intangible assets. Finally, the firm must estimate how much these e-commerce applications will add to the firm's profits.

As Fig. 6.1 illustrates, companies that are successful at using technology are finding that their intangible assets contribute to the huge gap between their market capitalization and the book value of their equity.

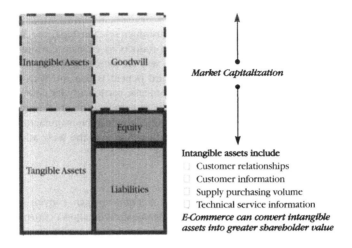

Market Capitalization

Intangible assets include
☐ Customer relationships
☐ Customer information
☐ Supply purchasing volume
☐ Technical service information
E-Commerce can convert intangible assets into greater shareholder value

Fig. 6.1   Strategic balance sheet analysis framework.

As Table 6.2 indicates, the e-commerce applications and the sources of incremental shareholder value tend to vary with the specific type of intangible asset. This table lists four of the many types of intangible assets that e-commerce can convert into increased shareholder value.

Table 6.2   E-commerce applications by intangible asset class.

Intangible asset	E-commerce application	Sources of value
Customer relationships	Web-based selling	Increased revenues, more efficient order fulfilment
Customer information	Personalization	Increased revenues per customer
Supply purchasing volume	Electronic procurement	Volume discounts, more efficient administration
Technical service information	Web-based self-service	Lower technical service costs

Customer relationships

Once a firm has established initial customer relationships, the Web is an efficient way to sell additional products to existing customers. Two benefits of using the Web in this way are increased revenues and lower incremental selling costs. A third benefit is that the Web can help streamline the order fulfillment process, particularly for complex products, by using artificial intelligence to guide customers through a process of ordering product configurations that can be manufactured. Cisco Systems has used this approach to selling over the Web, adding over $1.5bn to its profits in the process.

Customer information

Here is another intangible asset that e-commerce can convert into added shareholder value. Web-based personalization allows consumer marketers to use the Web to learn about a consumer's preferences and interests. When a consumer makes a purchase, the marketer can then use knowledge of these preferences to recommend additional items that people with similar interests have purchased. With personalization technology, such recommendations have a very high chance of being followed. This leads to dramatic increases in sales per customer. Levi Strauss' Website uses this technique, and has found that its customers accept 76% of the recommended additional items.

Supply purchasing volume

Many multidivisional firms purchase large volumes of supplies at the division level. Since these firms do not centralize purchasing, each division forges unique contractual arrangements with suppliers. In many cases, each division buys the same item from different suppliers. As a consequence, these firms leave money on the table by not purchasing these items from a single corporate location and not negotiating volume discounts with a preferred supplier. Electronic procurement is a Web-based application that enables firms to capture these volume discounts while streamlining the administration of the purchase process. Large firms such as General Electric are implementing electronic procurement systems, saving $1bn on its $5bn worth of corporate office supply purchases annually.

Technical service information

Companies that sell complex products typically offer technical service. Most companies that provide technical service keep records of each interaction between the technical service professionals and the customer. In many companies, these records are kept in file drawers. As a result, if a customer in one country has a particular technical problem with a product, it is unlikely that the customer service representative in that country will be familiar with all the solutions to that problem that may have been developed around the world. Therefore, there is a risk that technical service personnel may spend hours or days devising a solution to a problem that may have already been solved elsewhere within the company.

Web-based technical self-service enables customers to tap into the cumulative technical service experience of their vendor. It enhances customer satisfaction because technical problems are solved faster. It saves the vendor money by limiting the need to hire as many additional technical service people as a company grows. It also saves the vendor the cost of printing and mailing updated technical brochures and software patches to customers. Cisco's Web-based technical self-service application saved over $100mn in the latter category alone.

While each company must follow its own process of strategic balance sheet analysis, these examples should provide financial executives with a feeling for how successful users of e-commerce have proceeded.

COMPETITIVE OPPORTUNITY AND THREAT ANALYSIS

While executives are finding that strategic balance sheet analysis is a useful way to get started in thinking about how best to deploy e-commerce, this analysis should not be conducted in isolation.

As Fig. 6.2 illustrates, the Internet can change the structure of many industries. A new firm that uses the Internet to create competitive advantages can grow much faster than the average participant in that industry. An incumbent firm, growing at an average rate, faces an adaptation gap. This is the difference in growth rate between the incumbent and the new entrant. If the incumbent adapts its business model effectively, it can accelerate its rate of growth and survive the onslaught of the new competitor. If the incumbent adopts a wait and see attitude, it may be too late to adapt.

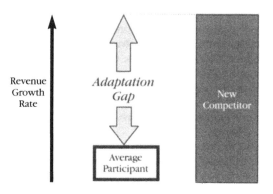

Fig. 6.2 Competitive adaptation gap analysis.

The bookselling industry is one example of this phenomenon. Amazon.com sells books, CDs, and videos over the Web. While Amazon.com has been growing at over 100% per year, Barnes & Noble and Borders are growing at under 10% annual rates. The stock market has rewarded Amazon.com with a market capitalization that is greater than the sum of Barnes & Noble's and Borders' combined market capitalization. Barnes & Noble chose to adapt, somewhat slowly, through a two-pronged strategy. First, the company began to sell books over the Web itself. Second, it purchased Amazon.com's chief book supplier, Ingram Book Group. It remains to be seen whether Barnes & Noble will be able to accelerate its revenue growth and impede the progress of Amazon.com.

As we noted earlier, executives must find ways to enhance the value of the firm's intangible assets. The competitive adaptation gap analysis suggests that executives must also analyze the strategies of new competitors, like Amazon.com, who can use the Internet to put the firm at a substantial competitive disadvantage. In fact, executives should also develop ideas for e-commerce applications that can put

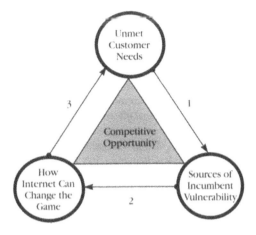

Fig. 6.3 Competitive opportunity analysis.

the firm in a position to accelerate its growth rate relative to these new entrants. Executives should also consider strategic moves that can position the advantages of the incumbent firm against the weaknesses of the new entrant.

While the majority of incumbent firms are likely to wait until a new entrant has established a beachhead, in every industry there will be a few firms that will take the initiative (and the risk) necessary to implement game-changing e-commerce applications ahead of their peers. Executives in these firms must create competitive opportunities.

As Fig. 6.3 suggests, there is an important sequence of activities that must be performed to identify valuable competitive opportunities. First, the firm must talk to customers in order to identify specific unmet needs with the industry's products. Amazon.com found that customers wished that there was a more efficient way to search, select, and take delivery of books. Office Depot found that small businesses were looking for a much more efficient way to select, take delivery, and pay for office supplies.

The next step in the analysis is to study competitors to understand where they would be vulnerable if they chose to offer a product that satisfied the customers' unmet needs. Amazon.com found that traditional bookstores could not stock all the titles in print, nor could they create an efficient way of matching a reader's interests with all the possible books in print. Office Depot found that many competing office superstores would be reluctant to sell over the Web because the Web channel would compete with in-store, catalog, direct and telephone sales forces. These incumbent methods of office supply distribution would not welcome the additional internal competition from a Website.

The final step in the competitive opportunity analysis is to think of ways that the Internet can change the game to favor your firm. More specifically, the challenge is to imagine a way that your firm can use the Internet to satisfy unmet customer needs in a way that will be difficult for competitors to copy. Amazon.com realized that selling books over the Web would enable consumers to select from a larger set of books, more efficiently, and take convenient delivery at a competitive price. Furthermore, given the high relative costs, lower selection, and relatively inefficient search process of traditional bookstores, Amazon.com would enjoy a sustainable competitive advantage.

Office Depot is hoping to achieve significant sales growth by using the Web as a parallel channel for distributing office supplies. It remains to be seen how effectively this company's Web-based selling of office supplies will work. Nevertheless, its experience represents a credible demonstration of the value of competitive opportunity analysis for an incumbent firm seeking to take the initiative in its industry.

E-COMMERCE RISK EVALUATION

The financial executive is particularly concerned about how e-commerce initiatives identified through the previous analyses may increase the risk of loss to the firm. In many cases, executives' fear about the additional risks that e-commerce introduces into the firm is as great as the absence of tools to help evaluate and manage such risks.

As Fig. 6.4 demonstrates, e-commerce introduces three new kinds of risk into the firm. While fraud has always been a problem, the Internet creates the potential for an unscrupulous purchasing agent to create bogus Web-based suppliers. If the firm is not aware of the fraud, the unscrupulous purchasing agent can create false transactions with the

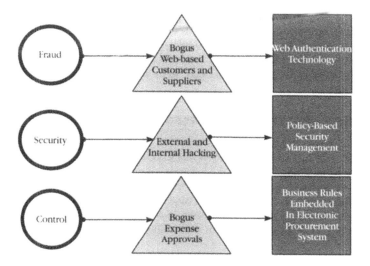

Fig. 6.4 E-commerce risk evaluation framework.

bogus Web-based supplier and use them to steal from the company. One solution to this problem is to use authentication technology.

While information security has always been a concern, e-commerce opens up the risk of information security breaches to a larger number of individuals both inside and outside the company. To combat such problems the policy-based network security management products offered by software firms enable companies to secure their information assets from theft and tampering in an integrated fashion.

Finally, e-commerce introduces new control problems. For example, an electronic procurement system streamlines the administration of the purchasing process. There is a danger that this streamlined process will open up opportunities for employees to obtain bogus approval for the purchase of valuable products and services.

Many electronic procurement system vendors offer firms the ability to embed business rules regarding approval of purchases into the electronic procurement system, thereby sustaining managerial controls.

Despite these technologies, the e-commerce risks are real. Executives must evaluate them diligently and take a cautious approach to the adoption of the technologies outlined above. We will examine in greater detail the procedures that executives can follow to identify the risks of e-commerce and take steps to protect their firms from loss.

ENTERPRISE VALUE ASSESSMENT

The research for this book reveals that there is nothing new about the method of financial analysis that executives apply to e-commerce projects. However, as Fig. 6.5 suggests, e-commerce applications present opportunities for financial executives to consider factors in their evaluations that are typically associated with mergers or stock buybacks, not information technology projects. In other words, some e-commerce projects can significantly boost shareholder value.

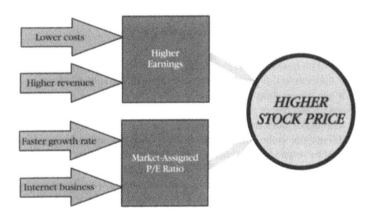

Fig. 6.5 Enterprise value assessment.

Executives attempt to quantify the cash flows associated with each e-commerce project. The costs of the project are typical of other information technology projects, although often the cost of the hardware and software is less than that of the Web consulting services. Further-more, the time frames for systems development should be dramatically shorter because in many cases, e-commerce applications are intended to be introduced to the market quickly and subsequently modified based on user feedback.

Nevertheless, the real benefits to the firm that must be measured have to do with two factors that influence growth in a firm's stock price. The first factor is the extent to which the e-commerce project enhances the firm's profits by lowering costs and/or increasing revenues. The second factor, particularly powerful in the case of e-commerce applications, is the extent to which the application increases the price/earnings ratio that the market assigns to the firm's earnings.

Certain e-commerce applications can cause the market to assign a much higher P/E ratio to the firm's expected earnings. Dramatic examples of such applications have become increasingly common. For example, when Zapata Corporation, a maker of fish extract, announced that it was going to purchase Internet companies, its stock promptly doubled. While such extreme examples are not likely to apply to traditional companies, they do indicate the extent to which companies are able to improve their market capitalization through investment in Internet subsidiaries. We will explore the specific steps required to make the sorts of investments in e-commerce applications that can both create value for customers and sustain high shareholder returns.

E-COMMERCE PORTFOLIO ANALYSIS

Once executives have completed the foregoing analysis, there is a need to integrate all the potential e-commerce applications and choose the ones that the firm will build. In order to make this choice, exec-utives need a framework that appropriately weighs the right factors and compares each potential e-commerce application using the same factors. Table 6.3 illustrates how such a framework might be deployed for a hypothetical set of five potential e-commerce applications.

While the data has been developed for purposes of illustration, the figure is useful for explaining the methodology used to evaluate a set of potential e-commerce applications. There are four evaluation criteria in this case. *Competitive shield* means how much the potential e-commerce project protects the firm from loss of market share to

Table 6.3 E-commerce portfolio analysis framework.

Ranked projects	Competitive shield	Minimize risk	Customer value add	Stock value add	Overall score
Weight	25	25	20	30	100
Project A	125	125	100	150	500
Project B	100	75	80	120	375
Project C	75	100	60	90	325
Project D	25	50	40	60	175
Project E	50	25	20	30	125

competitors. *Minimize risk* refers to the extent to which the project is conceived to limit the loss to the firm from fraud, security breaches, or weak controls. *Customer value add* measures the extent to which the project will cause the firm to do a better job of satisfying unmet customer needs. *Shareholder value add* refers to the extent to which the potential e-commerce application will enhance the firm's stock price.

The weights are an attempt to measure the relative importance of these four criteria in evaluating the potential e-commerce projects. This example places the least weight on *customer value add* and the most weight on *shareholder value add*. Each project is force ranked on each criterion and the weighted score is included in the table. The weighted scores are added and the projects are ranked in descending order of weighted score. This ranking may help firms with limited budgets to decide which e-commerce projects to fund and which to defer or cancel.

In the last two years, investors and managers have altered the way they perceive the Internet. In 1998, investors saw the Internet as a gold rush in which the biggest mistake was not to participate. Managers saw the Internet as a sharp knife about to be plunged into the heart of their business unless they reacted with an e-business strategy of their own.

Two years later investors and managers are less emotional about the Web. Managers view the Internet as a relatively cheap, wide-bandwidth global communications network, which – if used properly – can help them cut costs and/or increase revenues. Investors see that just as no "pure play dot-tel" firms emerged from the introduction of the telephone, few "pure play dot-coms" are likely to survive the use of the Internet as a business tool.

Since April 1999, we have seen three significant developments in the world of Internet business that help explain the changing managerial and investor perceptions about the Internet.

» Investors changed their methods of evaluating some Internet stocks.
» Investors recognized that Internet venture capital was not immune to losing money.
» Investment fads are going in and out of favor at an accelerating rate.

1. Investors changed their method of evaluating some Internet stocks

Prior to the April 2000 crash in Internet stocks, many investors bought them for one simple reason – their stock prices were going up. This so-called momentum approach to investing drove stock prices higher as more people invested trying to get a share of the new wealth.

People who were not directly involved in Internet business saw those who were lucky enough to own shares in Internet businesses get very rich very young. And the press was more than happy to document the stories of dot-com billionaires under the age of 30.

In a moment of crisis, it becomes clear that people are still ruled more strongly by their emotions than by their intellects. Investors who were laboring away at "normal" jobs felt the raw terror of missing out on the biggest gold rush of their careers. While their minds were telling them that many dot-com businesses were not likely to earn a profit, their emotions were telling them that they had no chance of winning unless they owned a ticket to the Internet lottery. The fear of being left behind the dot-com gold rush was just such a moment of crisis. People decided that the best way to make the most money quickly was to purchase shares in stocks that were going up the fastest. Day traders would see a particular stock referred to on CNBC and buy shares in the company without any knowledge of the company's operations.

But emotions were unable to snuff out logic altogether. Logic suggested that many of the dot-com stocks were producing very ugly income statements and balance sheets. Simply put, the companies were losing huge amounts of money and were using up cash faster than they could generate it from operations. The only way the companies could stay in business was to convince investors to drink the dot-com Kool Aid (i.e. to buy more shares of dot-com stock).

How did they do this? Since traditional methods of keeping score made dot-coms look like they were losers, the dot-coms made up new accounting methods that made them look like they were winners. One of the most popular of these metrics was "eyeballs." Dot-coms claimed that they were succeeding because they were able to attract more and more unique visitors to their Websites. The dot-coms focused initially on winning the eyeball wars, and assumed that they could reap profits later.

The new dot-com math helped to keep the air inside the bubble for an extended period of time. While there were many warnings that eventually things had to come back to earth, the press was full of articles about the distinction between the old economy and the new. These articles gave the impression that things were different now; in the new economy, all trees grow to the sky. People kept holding onto their dot-com stocks believing that if the doubters proved to be right, they could get out in time. At one point near the top, the NASDAQ climbed over 5000 and some journalists were asking how soon the NASDAQ would exceed the DJIA, which at the time was trading in the 11,000 to 12,000 range.

Ultimately, the dot-com bubble was popped by an analysis of the most fundamental of all business measures – the cash burn rate. Simply put, a big chunk of the well-known dot-com companies had no more than a few months of cash remaining before they would run out of cash. This analysis flipped investors' emotional coin – from fear of losing out to fear of losing it all. The result of this emotional flip of the coin was a selling panic that has wiped out about 90% of the stock market value in many of the dot-com companies.

Priceline is a fine example of this phenomenon. This company had established a Website that let travelers bid on airline tickets out of airlines' unsold seat inventories. Priceline stock peaked at $162 in

April 1999, but it lost so much money and failed so consistently to meet expectations of its financial performance that investors simply abandoned the stock – and stock declined to $6 in November 2000, a stunning 96% loss.

The April 2000 dot-com crash highlighted the failure of the new dot-com math. It also underlined the need for application of traditional valuation measures as intellectual justification for Internet stock valuations.

2. Investors recognized that Internet venture capital was not immune to losing money

Many investors believed that the dot-com companies – a subset of e-commerce which also includes b2b – were the drivers of the other eight Internet business segments (see Chapter 2 "Nine Internet business segments" [no.6]). Their view was "as go the dot-coms, so go the other Internet business segments." Throughout much of 1999, this observation was astute. However, in the summer of 1999, the first cracks in the dot-com armor began to appear. Business-to-consumer was increasingly perceived by venture capital firms as low-margin business even as some investors continued to pour money into the 15th online pet food provider.

At that time, some venture capital firms began to believe that b2b was an even bigger and more profitable opportunity than b2c. While CMGI had focused primarily on b2c, and its stock price had appreciated very nicely, a newly public venture capital firm, Internet Capital Group (ICGE), was focusing on the hot new business-to-business area.

Although the summer of 1999 was a fairly quiet period for initial public offerings, ICGE was able to go public albeit without a booming first-day pop. As investors began to realize that ICGE was focused on the hot new market, its stock price proceeded to climb 2000% from $10 in July 1999 to $212 by the end of December 1999. However, this was not to last. Unfortunately for those who may have had the misfortune of investing in ICGE at its peak, the year 2000 marked an almost uninterrupted decline in ICGE from $212 at the beginning of January 2000 to $6 in November 2000.

Why the sharp rise and fall of ICGE? A key element was the market-moving power of the momentum investors who feverishly bought

ICGE stock during its climb to $212 and then just as feverishly sold the stock on its way down throughout much of 2000. This happened because it is almost impossible to analyze the value of the portfolios of Internet venture capital firms, because so many portfolio companies are privately held with few publicly traded peers with which their value can be compared. As a result, the stock prices of publicly traded venture capital firms are excellent indicators of investor sentiment within the sector – and votes on the level of missionary zeal which their CEOs have managed to inspire. However, the stock prices are not good measures of the inherent value of the firms' portfolio companies.

While the case of ICGE has some unique elements, it is indicative of the overall trend in Internet venture capital – a significant decline in investment returns. As *Net Profit* pointed out in April 1999, Internet venture capital returns are subject to wide fluctuation. While venture capital firms have generated a long-term average rate of return of roughly 36%, the second-quarter 2000 performance was about a tenth of the long-term average, at about 4%. This stunningly low rate of return probably foreshadows a few quarters of significant negative returns in the world of Internet venture capital. Anecdotal evidence suggests that even the most highly respected venture firms invested in dot-coms that have collapsed in areas such as pet food, toys, and restaurant reservations. In fact, leading Internet-content publications such as *The Industry Standard*, *Upside* and *Red Herring* have developed layoff trackers and dot-com graveyards just to keep track of all the failed businesses backed by many of the leading venture funds.

In the next several quarters, the forces compressing these returns are likely to exceed the forces expanding them. In particular, the sharp decline in the number of successful Initial Public Offerings (IPOs) since April 2000, the tremendous losses suffered by dot-com investors, and the growth in the number of funds exceeding $1bn are likely to place downward pressure on venture capital returns. This growth in high-end funds is particularly important because it signals a tremendous pressure to invest large amounts of money rapidly, which in turn reinforces the tendency of some venture funds simply to follow the latest trend without conducting sufficiently rigorous analysis before investing.

3. Investment fads are going in and out of favor at an accelerating rate

The rate of change in investment fads has accelerated. This acceleration has made it particularly challenging for investors in public equities. While b2c e-commerce retained significant popularity among investors from 1996 to April 2000, subsequent investment fads enjoyed much shorter half lives. For example, b2b e-commerce became very popular in the summer of 1999 and lost popularity in April 2000. Interestingly, b2b regained some investor interest after the second quarter 2000 operating results of a few industry leaders – such as Ariba and Commerce One – were announced. Other investment fads such as wireless and optical networking experienced even more rapid waxing and waning in popularity.

Although the half lives of these investment fads have shortened, they tend to share certain common patterns. Investment fads begin and end with a poster child. The press plays an important role here in creating and destroying investment fads. The press seeks out a colorful person who can represent an entire investment sector. For b2c e-commerce, the poster child is Amazon's bellowed-laughing Jeff Bezos, for b2b e-commerce it's ex-GE executive and FreeMarket's CEO, Glen Meakem, and for optical networking the poster child is sports-car loving Nortel CEO, John Roth.

Yet the press can destroy an investment fad just as quickly – for example, Jeff Bezos, *Time*'s man of the year in 1999, submitted himself to harsh grilling on CNN's *MoneyLine* only a few months later after posting disappointing financial results. Since *Time* and CNN share the same parent company, Bezos proved a convenient demonstration of the synergies between the print and cable TV media and a compelling example of the central role that the press plays creating and destroying investment fads.

While the press is an important catalyst for investment fads, the key enablers are the financial markets. The venture capital firms prime the pumps for the investment fads by piling into each new investment sector. In general, there is one venture capital firm that is willing to lead the pack and the others rapidly follow. The trigger that often encourages the others to follow the lead dog is that lead dog's previous track record of successful "exits." For example, if Benchmark Capital turns a $4mn pre-IPO investment in eBay into $2bn post-IPO then other venture capitalists will tend to want to pile into the same sector that Benchmark chooses next.

Venture capitalists cannot achieve their ends alone. They must act in concert with the investment banks that underwrite IPOs. If the IPO market is hot for a particular category, such as optical networking, then other venture capital companies and investment banks will be eager to invest and underwrite, respectively, in that hot category. Unfortunately, as the half lives of category heat get shorter and shorter, there is an increasing risk that lagging investors will be entering a category just as the IPO window for that category is shutting down.

For example, in optical networking, one company, Corvis, was able to go public and quickly gain a market capitalization in excess of $20bn despite having no revenues. But this was before the fever for optical networking cooled. When Nortel Networks announced in the third quarter 2000 that the growth in its optical networking business had slowed down slightly, the deceleration in growth caused many leading optical networking firms to see their market capitalization decline 30% to 40% on the day of Nortel's earnings report.

Venture capitalists can have a powerful impact on pre-IPO companies if their priorities change. For example, pre-IPO companies can also find themselves abandoned due to a change in their provider's position. Priceline suffered a stream of earnings disappointments and, as a result, venture capitalists abandoned the sector entirely out of a fear of losing their entire investment in the sector (and a parallel desire to limit that loss by turning off the cash spigot.)

In sum, the actions of venture capital prime the pumps for investment fads, so it is important to anticipate what is likely to happen in this sector. Internet venture capital is a volatile business and it is heading into a downturn. The result is that a few years from now, the venture capital industry will emerge with fewer competitors, who are likely to approach venture investing in a more conservative fashion.

In the interim there is much damage yet to be done. Ventures that have yet to go public will find their funding cut off and most will close. Today's hot optical networking sector could lose 90% of the ventures that are now being funded. The venture firms that focused solely on the hot new sectors will struggle and possibly close down. The few firms that performed independent analysis of sectors and companies and acted accordingly may – if their analysis proves correct – capture the opportunities in the next upturn.

Individual investors should stay away from sectors of the stock market that are rising rapidly unless they have reason to believe that the fundamental business performance is likely to justify these market price increases. If the stock market is driving prices higher despite weak fundamental business performance, investors should resist the temptation to participate. It is inevitable that the stock price will eventually drop to a level no higher than its operating performance can justify.

In Practice

What does it take to profit from the Internet? This chapter provides the answer by presenting case studies of e-leaders, including:

» US Cavalry;
» Nokia; and
» NTT DoCoMo;

Three cases – one from the US, one from Finland, and one from Japan – illustrate the unique skills of, and challenges facing, e-leaders around the world.

US CAVALRY GOES ONLINE

Based in Radcliff, KY, US Cavalry is a retailer of military and law enforcement uniforms and accessories, with 290 employees. The company retails survival and outdoor clothing and equipment, action sports equipment and collectables. It was founded in June 1973 to capitalize on the less than convenient service and relatively narrow uniform and accessory selection available at military bases. US Cavalry offered convenience and a wide selection of products where military base stores provided a limited product selection open a few hours a day.

The enterprise started with one store in Kentucky and over the years opened up four additional stores in Kentucky, North Carolina, Georgia and Texas. In 1975 US Cavalry distributed 1800 catalogs to potential customers, and by 1998 was distributing 7.5 million catalogs annually, listing 4500 items in each of its 1998 catalogs.

In 1995 Randy Acton, US Cavalry's CEO, decided to go online. He was convinced that the Internet was the wave of the future and he wanted his company to be there. Acton registered the uscav.com URL and built a preliminary Website. This included a US Cavalry home page, a version of the complete catalog, and a toll-free number that visitors could call to order the printed catalog.

Acton found that the Website generated 5000 requests a month for the catalog, but despite the additional cost of printing and mailing more catalogs, US Cavalry was not getting many more orders. Acton realized that he needed to curb those people who ordered the catalog without placing orders. So he notified visitors that everything that was in the catalog was on the Website. Those who were more comfortable ordering from a catalog than using the Web were free to do so. However, the company instituted a new policy that required them to pay for the privilege. As a result, only people who intended to place an order would request the catalog. US Cavalry still did not want its customers using the Web to place orders because Acton was concerned that the security issues had not been satisfactorily resolved. Customers who decided not to order the catalog could use the Web site to decide what they wanted and place the order via telephone.

In October 1997, US Cavalry decided to take the next step in using the Web. Acton had been following the strategies of retailers whom he respected, such as L.L. Bean and Eddie Bauer, who were further along in building Websites. But Acton remained concerned that the Web was not secure, and the last thing he wanted to do was to risk the excellent customer relationships that he had built up over 20 years by putting his business on an insecure Website. When he heard about VeriSign and its software product shopping.org, he realized that he could confidently put his business on the Web without risking his customer relationships. VeriSign's technology would enable his customers to secure the confidential payment information that they would send to US Cavalry's Web site. As a result, Acton felt that customers would not be scared away from conducting electronic commerce at uscav.com.

That same month, Acton went ahead and put the Website into electronic commerce mode. He was determined to make the site fast, secure, and easy to use. He made the site fast by cutting away unnecessary elements such as pictures of products, substituting keywords. He made the site secure with the VeriSign technology. He made the site easy to use by installing an easy-to-use search engine that let visitors search for merchandise by using a variety of search keys.

The team of people involved in the project varied depending on the project phase. In the beginning, Acton and his director of marketing, Sam Young, developed ideas for how the Website would operate. When they decided what they wanted it to look like, they co-ordinated an internal MIS programmer with an external layout artist who had HTML programming expertise. Once the site was built, US Cavalry received extensive feedback from customers that enabled the firm to change the system, making it easier to use and faster.

In October 1998, US Cavalry was working on creating a linkage between its Web front-end ordering and its back-end fulfillment systems. Prior to initiating this linkage phase, the company had simply printed out orders on paper that had been received via the Web and handed the paper orders on to its traditional order fulfillment process.

US Cavalry has invested some people and analytical time into responding to and analyzing the data that it gets from its Website.

For example, it has dedicated people specifically to answering questions that customers pose via the e-mail system linked to its Website. Customers tend to ask technical product and general customer service questions.

In addition, US Cavalry receives extensive data from its Internet service provider pertaining to activity on its Website, and is able to analyze this data to find out which products are selling the best, how customer preferences are shifting, and other important insights that help the company enhance the Website's ability to generate higher revenues. One valuable insight that US Cavalry has extracted from this analysis is that when a visitor searches a Web portal such as Yahoo! for an item that US Cavalry sells, such as army boots, it is highly profitable to pay a the Web portal to ferry the searcher to the US Cavalry Website, a practice first touched on in Chapter 6. The company has found that this linkage with the search engine is much more profitable than a banner advertisement on the Web portal.

US Cavalry generated other valuable insights as a result of feedback from customers and its own internal idea generation process. For example, it has learned that if the customer is given something "free" with the order, then the average order size will increase. US Cavalry's average Internet order of $105 is already higher than its average catalog order of $79. A typical promotion to motivate higher average orders was to give a customer a $150 pair of leather boots if that customer placed an order over $500. In addition to increasing the size of the average order, this promotion reduced excess inventory.

Acton recommends that any retailer considering a Website becomes familiar with direct marketing, for if a retailer is accustomed to selling its product in a store only, the direct marketing aspect of the Web will come as a shock. The Web is much like selling a product on TV with an 800 number. To operate a direct-marketing fulfillment process, a firm must have the ability to pick, pack and ship an order from the warehouse very efficiently. Acton had this experience already, due to his large catalog business. Going on the Web only changed the medium by which the order was received.

Acton continues to get orders from both the printed catalog and the Web, each of these media promoting the other. However, US Cavalry is having much better results with its Website than a typical direct marketer gets from direct mail, 50% of its orders coming from new Web customers. The typical new-customer yield of direct mail programs is 2%.

KEY INSIGHTS

The success of US Cavalry's Website is partially a result of its ability to overcome some of the more common challenges facing companies seeking to profit from the Web. Here are four such pitfalls.

Lack of management commitment

Many corporate change initiatives follow a similar pattern. Management starts the initiative with fanfares and enthusiasm. A team is formed and begins work with ambitious goals and tight project plans. When the first deadline passes without meeting the target, management distances itself from the project. The drive for success is replaced with a run for cover. The project manager disappears from the company, and the project is never discussed again. Soon thereafter a new fad comes along to capture the attention of senior management and the cycle begins anew.

There is a real danger that a Web project will fall victim to this cycle. The best way to prevent this outcome is not to get started with the project until there are sufficient facts available to make reliable plans and to set realistic expectations. Fundamentally, if a project is really going to increase the value of the company's shares, then senior management has a personal incentive to assure its success. It is the Web application team's job to ensure that the project rests on a firm foundation of facts.

Unclear project objectives

If you don't know where you are going, any road will get you there. Yet many projects start off with great enthusiasm because they borrow their wind from the almost overpowering weather front of industry hype. As a result, some projects get started without a well-thought-out set of objectives that make sense in the context of the company. Sometimes this happens because people familiar with the technology allow their enthusiasm for the Web and its capabilities to overwhelm the voices that focus on business benefits.

The best way to overcome the problem of unclear objectives is for the CEO and the Web application team to assure themselves that the project objectives are specific, measurable, achievable, and yet ambitious. The CEO can develop such objectives if other companies have achieved similar objectives and the CEO believes that his firm has the ability and the desire to accomplish such objectives.

Absence of internal teamwork

If teamwork is not a value that is widely practiced within a company, then it will be difficult for the firm to embrace teamwork in creating a Web application. If a firm's departments are better at battling each other than at working together to create value for the customer, then it may not make sense for the firm to undertake a Web application. If the CEO does not encourage departments to work together under normal business circumstances, it may be asking too much for the CEO to suddenly begin to encourage effective teamwork.

Therefore, a company should not undertake a Web application unless it normally encourages teamwork across the various operating units and departments of the company. Web applications tend to require very smooth interactions among different organizations. If the firm is accustomed to such interactions, then implementing a Web application will proceed relatively smoothly. Even so, the CEO may need to offer specific incentives to Web application team members to encourage them to work on the team and to meet the project objectives that have removed them from their "normal" jobs or given them additional burdens.

Overly ambitious plans

Projects can founder if they try to do too much. For example, if a project team decides it will work for two to three years before a massive systems overhaul is complete, there is a danger that much money will be spent and too little in the way of tangible benefits will be achieved.

If the project is rolled out in phases, each of which produces tangible benefits, then the project will be able to sustain momentum.

NOKIA NO LONGER WALKS ON WATER

After enjoying years of praise from analysts, Nokia's June 2001 announcement of slowing growth has hurt the company's credibility, and it shows that mobile data transmission is so far not a significant market.

In June 2000, the vision associated with this sector appeared compelling. As Europeans surfed the Web via their mobile phones, a new generation of speedy, data-friendly handsets would fly off store shelves. Jorma Ollila, chief of Finland's Nokia, the world's largest and most profitable mobile-phone maker, embraced this idea enthusiastically.

Then, on June 12, 2001 Nokia shocked investors with a profits warning, slashing second-quarter sales growth estimates in half, to less than 10%. The "sell" orders on Nokia's stock that followed cut $31bn off the company's market capitalization in one day. The suddenly gloomy Ollila blamed a deterioration "driven by economic uncertainty, the ongoing technology transition, and less aggressive marketing by the operators." Translation: Europe's economy was in worse shape than expected, and mobile data transmission, the big hope of companies like Nokia and its next-door rival, Sweden's Ericsson, has so far proved a significant disappointment. The networks to provide the promised mobile data services were not expected to be in place until late summer 2001 at the earliest. The phones will not be available soon. And in Europe, virtually everybody who wants an ordinary digital cell phone has one.

Until Ollila's announcement, investors assumed Nokia would somehow continue to post strong revenue and profit gains, despite the challenges facing rivals such as Ericsson and Motorola. Until recently,

Nokia predicted a global market of 550 million cell phones by the end of 2001, with its own share at 40% of the total. In June 2001, Nokia estimated 2001 demand at 405 million phones. Analysts at Merrill Lynch estimate demand will be 390 million.

Nokia says its earlier optimism reflected what it was seeing in the first quarter of 2001 and that it did not expect America's problems to spread so quickly. Still, the change in outlook is "a blow to Nokia's credibility," according to Mark Davies Jones, managing director for telecommunications equipment research at Schroder Salomon Smith Barney in London.

Delays from Nokia are contributing to the mobile Internet market slowdown. The company's phones for the next stage, so-called 2.5G, are late. This leaves customers like Vodafone Group PLC with high-speed networks in place and few handsets to sell. Analysts see a decline in Nokia profits of 12% in 2001, to around $4.3bn on sales of $26bn.

The environment is looking increasingly grim with the European market reaching saturation, as much as 70% of the population now owning phones. Adding to the pressure, many European cellular telephone operators struggling with large debts are cutting the subsidies that spurred handset sales. In April 2001, world leader Vodafone began cutting these subsidies. Meanwhile, the drop in European demand makes Nokia increasingly dependent on sales in more price-competitive markets like China and Egypt.

With nearly three-quarters of its revenues coming from handsets, Nokia had significant hopes that existing customers would upgrade their phones to get faster Internet access, including services such as mobile air ticketing and driving directions. However, as Europe's phone companies have been forced to scale back spending on 2.5G and 3G networks, the resultant delays are cooling a once torrid market. Merrill Lynch analyst Adnaan Ahmad, for example, believes that the golden years of subscriber growth and mobile capital expenditures of the 1990s are not likely to recur.

This trend to slower or declining demand growth will hurt Nokia, which had counted on an increase in its telecommunications infrastructure business to offset a drop in consumer handsets. The company had been steadily taking market share in infrastructure by offering about $4bn in loans in 2000 to heavily indebted wireless operators. Now, it admits its infrastructure sales will grow only as fast as the market, a big shock to investors. Davies Jones noted that Nokia has not been taking market share in telecommunications infrastructure in the same way as it had taken share in handsets. A further problem is that as more telecommunications companies strike deals to share the cost of building 3G networks, demand for equipment is likely to fall. Nokia is moving some production to lower-cost countries such as Mexico and China, and it will likely curtail loans to operators. But what it really needs to do is deliver the promised benefits of the mobile Internet. Only then will Nokia regain its star status.

KEY INSIGHTS

Nokia turned itself into a wireless dynamo in the 1990s; however, its rapid fall from grace suggests four important lessons for companies aspiring to sustain e-leadership.

Anticipate changing patterns of demand

Nokia became somewhat overconfident in its strength and was somewhat blind-sided by a significant demand drop. Nevertheless, it appears clear that the dot-com stock market crash which began in April 2000 provided ample warning of a future slowdown in demand. While the connection between the stock market crash and a decline in demand for cell phones may not have been clear initially, it should have become obvious to senior managers at Nokia that the absence of profitability in many consumer-oriented e-commerce businesses would ultimately make it difficult for these wireless service demand drivers to continue indefinitely.

One key lesson from this case is that e-leaders must monitor early warning indicators that could help them anticipate changes in demand patterns.

Envision multiple paths of technological evolution

Nokia may have been too confident that the market would unstintingly adopt its vision for how technology would evolve. As a result, when the market did not adopt the technologies as Nokia had anticipated, the company was caught unprepared for the demand for 2.5G phones. Had Nokia anticipated multiple paths of technological evolution rather than the one that would be most favorable to itself, it is more likely that it would have been in a stronger position to respond to the specific technologies that became popular as capital from wireless service providers dried up.

Simply put, it is important for an aspiring e-leader to have a strong vision of how technology will evolve – however, it is equally important to test that vision against the potentially jarring reality that customers may not share that vision (at least in the short to medium term).

Sustain intellectual humility

Implicit in the first two case studies is an underlying lesson that often among the most challenging and potentially overwhelming side effects of being very successful, it is a growing sense of overconfidence that leads to failure.

Firms that have succeeded through several waves of new technology, such as Microsoft, have created management mechanisms that keep themselves from the blinding effects of overconfidence. Examples of such management mechanisms include:

- » independent quarterly measurement of customer satisfaction and linkage of all employee bonuses to increases in the overall customer satisfaction score;
- » brutally honest new-product self-evaluations that identify what went wrong with a new-product initiative, with suggestions for improvements in the future; and
- » customer usability laboratories in which developers of new products can study how customers actually use products under development, so that problems with these products can be identified and solved, and unmet customer needs discovered and addressed with new products.

React quickly to market changes

A final important lesson from the Nokia case is that the sooner a firm can react to a decline in demand – for example, by cutting its operating costs - the better protected that firm's shareholders will be. One of the reasons why Nokia shareholders knocked $31bn off its stock market capitalization following the June 2001 earnings announcement is that they were so surprised by the declining demand.

If Nokia had done a better job of anticipating the sluggish demand using the methods discussed above, it is likely that it would have reduced its costs and moved its production to lower-cost locations such as Mexico and China more rapidly. Nokia's management brought on itself a more profound problem through its unwillingness to adapt in a more timely way to changing market conditions - a loss of investor credibility.

While it is perhaps understandable that management would hope things would improve up until the last minute, the lack of responsibility inherent in this slow response suggests that perhaps investors will need new management in place in order to regain confidence in Nokia's future. The inability of the company's management to anticipate this outcome suggests poor judgment in the face of challenging conditions of declining demand.

DYNAMIC DOCOMO: NTT'S WIRELESS WORLD LEADER

Takeshi Natsuno's i-mode service is extremely popular in Japan – however, some analysts wonder how well i-mode could be adopted in other countries.

Natsuno, the original thinker behind the i-mode mobile-Internet service, learned the business the hard way. In 1996, he helped create Hypernet, Japan's first free Internet service provider, which expected to profit from selling advertising. Users were very interested in the enterprise, which grew rapidly the first year – too rapidly, as it turned out. Although Hypernet tried to keep up with the volume by putting in the latest technology, it was still fraught with operating problems. Corporate advertisers soon began leaving Hypernet. Natsuno himself quit in mid-1997, and the business closed its doors in December 1997.

Hypernet's unsuccessful outcome provided valuable lessons that Natsuno, 36, took to his next job – helping NTT's DoCoMo launch a wireless Internet business. Among those lessons: slow technology is better than no technology (especially if the technology is easy to use), and do not rely on advertisements. Instead, charge subscription fees and form partnerships with content providers that can also earn revenue by offering information services tailored for a small screen. Natsuno notes that telecommunications firms generally think of launching services unilaterally, never with partners. In Natsuno's view, unilaterally launching services does not work on the Internet.

DoCoMo adopted Natsuno's business strategy, which has generated attractive returns. In June 2001, for example, i-mode ranked as the world's first commercially viable mobile-Internet service. Between its launch in February 1999 and June 2001, i-mode had signed up 24 million subscribers, who contributed $2.8bn in revenue to DoCoMo in the year ended March 31, 2001 – an 840% increase over 1999. DoCoMo also posted profits of $3bn in fiscal 2001, a 45% jump from 2000.

Currently DoCoMo hopes to apply the lessons it learned from Natsuno in taking i-mode global. But not everyone is convinced i-mode is the model to adopt. European and American critics suggest that the mobile-Internet in Japan is largely focused on entertainment sites, such as music, animation downloads, services that locate the nearest karaoke bars and the best windsurf beaches. These services, while appealing to young people, may not be the best for corporate customers. As of July 2001, it was a difficult time to convince investors that wireless offered high returns. Europe, despite its interest in cell phones, was still recovering from its failed experiment with a mobile data service known as Wireless Application Protocol (WAP). And European wireless operators had taken on massive debt, the legacy of overspending on acquisitions and next-generation cellular licenses in the great rush to stake out wireless territory.

The US was not a booming wireless market, either. While more Americans were buying cell phones and logging on via wireless devices, the market remained fragmented, due to different service platforms.

Even so, some aspects of i-mode were expected to infiltrate the next generation of wireless services emerging outside Japan. And DoCoMo was investing in wireless carriers to help achieve this objective. In the US DoCoMo spent $9.8bn for a 16% share in AT&T Wireless, and plans to launch an i-mode-type service in Seattle in 2002. In the Netherlands, DoCoMo paid $4.5bn for 15% of KPN and plans to roll out parts of i-mode in Germany in late 2001, and in the Netherlands in 2002.

AT&T Wireless and KPN will introduce i-mode's user-friendly, packet-switched network, which lets subscribers tap into an always-on connection without dialing up. These partner-companies are also planning to copy i-mode's micropayment system, allowing content providers to charge low monthly fees that are collected as part of the carrier's monthly bill. DoCoMo has attracted nearly 2000 official content providers who charge $1 to $3 for services such as music and horoscopes. The point is not to replace the main Web's content, but to offer content specially designed for people who are traveling, such as simple games or news briefs.

However, outside Japan, many seem uncomfortable adopting the key element behind i-mode's success: its emphasis on simple, entertaining content. European and American service providers offer little more than banking, news, and travel information aimed at business users. Jeffry Funk, a mobile-Internet expert at Japan's Kobe University, for example, believes that the West has focused on the wrong set of items and still does not understand what drives the demand for i-mode. Funk thinks users are not as serious as service providers think they are, and that they would be willing to pay for fun content.

Europeans argue that the type of whimsical entertainment featured on i-mode appeals only to the Japanese. Arian Dorrestijn, an analyst at Rabobank in Amsterdam, for instance, notes that when he looks at what is successful with i-mode in Japan, he is not impressed. However, DoCoMo's Natsuno believes users everywhere will want a variety of content and services on their handsets. In his view, if a user can read the headlines, check all e-mail, and play games on a simple phone, there is no reason why the user would not do so. He is convinced that, if the European and American operators heed his advice, they could recreate i-mode's success in Japan. He acknowledges that the mobile-Internet will never replace PC-based services. In an increasingly mobile world, however, it could become the communication tool of choice for everyone – from teenagers in platform shoes to corporate warriors who just might want to search Zagat's for a good restaurant or check the latest baseball scores.

KEY INSIGHTS

The DoCoMo case highlights some of the key elements, including those below, which drive leading e-business firms' market leadership.

Understand the consumer

DoCoMo clearly developed a strong understanding of what consumers in Japan were looking for in this information service and was able to add new features that led to rapid market penetration.

Make the technology simple, robust and ubiquitous

DoCoMo was able to introduce a technology that suited the application – it was ubiquitous, simple to use, inexpensive to deliver, and always on. In this sense, the company did not overengineer its network, thereby making it too expensive to deliver the consumer benefits of its service.

Provide content that is simple and widely appealing

DoCoMo's insight into its consumers enabled it to partner with the right content providers and to add to its services in a way that would expand the number of users of the service. Furthermore, the decision to sell its service at a very low price encouraged widespread adoption and frequent daily use.

Cut attractive revenue sharing deals with content providers

DoCoMo's decision to take a 9% cut of the content revenues proved to be an equitable and profitable sharing of the revenue streams with content providers.

The DoCoMo case also suggests some important challenges, some of which are listed below, which will need to be overcome if the company is to achieve its ambition of carrying its i-mode service to Europe and the US.

» A sufficient number of consumers in Europe and the US may not find an i-mode-like service appealing.
» The technological infrastructure needed to deliver such a service reliably may be too expensive to implement profitably.
» It may be difficult to find content partners who can deliver the right services with the needed level of quality and price.
» Infrastructure partners may lack the financial and technological capabilities to help DoCoMo deliver the service.

SOME CONCLUSIONS

The three case studies analyzed here highlight some important general lessons for companies aspiring to be e-leaders. The first is that a successful business depends on creating value for customers. The winner in the market place is able to offer the best value proposition to consumers and to sustain the superiority of its offering, as competitors introduce new products and as new technologies threaten the existing distribution of market power.

The second key lesson of these cases is that technology must not drive the creation of a new product, in the sense of forcing consumers to adopt new technologies that do not create a compelling new value proposition. Another way of looking at this is that there are countless case studies of technologies that were imposed on customers who ultimately rejected them in favor of the best value proposition. E-leaders find the technology that delivers superior customer value.

Finally, e-leaders maintain their intellectual humility – recognizing that success in one technology round does not confer a limitless horizon of future success. Rather, e-leaders understand that success can lead to failure if success creates intellectual rigidity that causes the firm not to adapt to changing customer needs, upstart competitors and new technologies.

Key Concepts and Thinkers

There are many thinkers whose concepts form the foundation of the Internet. The lexicon of *E-Leaders* covers these concepts by exploring how their inventors developed them through their careers.

The key concepts related to e-leadership can be understood through a description of the careers of the Internet's progenitors, given below in alphabetical, and no other, order.

ANDREESEN, MARC

Marc Andreesen was a student and part-time assistant at the National Center for Supercomputing Applications (NCSA) at the University of Illinois when the World Wide Web began to take off. His position at NCSA allowed him to become very familiar with the Internet. Like just about everyone else who was involved with it, he also became familiar with the Web. Most of the browsers available then were for Unix machines, which were expensive. This meant that the Web was mostly used by academics and engineers who had access to such machines. The user interfaces of available browsers also tended to be not very user-friendly, which also hindered the spread of the Web. Marc decided to develop a browser that was easier to use and more graphically rich.

In 1992, Andreesen recruited fellow NCSA employee, Eric Bina, to help with his project. The two worked tirelessly. They called their new browser Mosaic, and it was much more sophisticated graphically than other browsers of the time. Like these it was designed to display HTML documents, but new formatting tags like "center" were included.

Especially important was the inclusion of the "image" tag, which allowed inclusion of images on Web pages. Earlier browsers allowed the viewing of pictures, but only as separate files. Mosaic made it possible for images and text to appear on the same page. Mosaic also sported a graphical interface with clickable buttons that let users navigate easily and controls that enabled them to scroll through text with ease. Another innovative feature was the hyperlink. In earlier browsers hypertext links had reference numbers that the user typed in to navigate to the linked document. Hyperlinks allowed the user to simply click on a link to retrieve a document.

In early 1993, Mosaic was posted for download on NCSA's servers. It was immediately popular. Within weeks tens of thousands of people had downloaded the software. The original version was for Unix. Andreesen and Bina quickly put together a team to develop PC and Mac versions, which were released in the late spring of the same year. With Mosaic now available for more popular platforms, its popularity skyrocketed. More users meant a bigger Web audience. The bigger audiences spurred the creation of new content, which in turn further increased the audience on the Web and so on. As the number of users on the Web increased, the browser of choice was Mosaic, and so its distribution increased accordingly.

By December 1993, Mosaic's growth was so great that it made the front page of the *New York Times* business section. The article concluded that Mosaic was perhaps an application program so different and so obviously useful that it could create a new industry from scratch. NCSA administrators were quoted in the article, but there was no mention of either Andreesen or Bina. Marc realized that when he was through with his studies NCSA would take over Mosaic for itself. So when he graduated in December 1993, he left and moved to Silicon Valley in California.

Andreesen settled in Palo Alto, and soon met Jim Clark, who had founded Silicon Graphics, Inc. He had money and connections. The two began talking about a possible new start-up company; others were brought into the discussions and it was decided that they would start an Internet company. Marc contacted old friends still working for NCSA and enticed a group of them to become the engineering team for the new company. In mid-1994, Mosaic Communications Corporation was officially incorporated in Mountain View, CA, and Andreesen became the vice president of technology of the new company.

The new team's mandate was to create a product to surpass the original Mosaic. They had to start from scratch because the original had been created in university time with university money, and so belonged exclusively to the university. The team worked furiously.

The new product would need a name. Eventually, the name Netscape was adopted. It would also need a price structure. At first, a plan to charge $99 for the browser, $5,000 for the basic server, and $25,000 for the commercial server (which included Secure Socket Layer Technology, or SSL, and could encrypt sensitive information such as credit card numbers) was considered. It was then decided to charge $1,500 for the baseline server and $5,000 for the commercial server.

Pricing for the browser was a complex question. Andreesen and others knew that the key to success would be making Netscape ubiquitous on the Web. Andreesen recalls:

"That was the way to get the company jump-started, because that just gives you essentially a broad platform to build off of. It's basically a Microsoft lesson, right? If you get ubiquity, you have a lot of options, a lot of ways to benefit from that. You can get paid by the product you are ubiquitous on, but you can also get paid on products that benefit as a result. One of the fundamental lessons is that market share now equals revenue later, and if you don't have market share now, you are not going to have revenue later. Another fundamental lesson is that whoever gets the volume does win in the end. Just plain wins."

They decided to adopt a "free but not free" price structure for the browser. It would be free for students and educators; $39 for everybody else. In reality, nearly everyone had free access when Netscape was released. Beta versions were available for free, and new beta versions came out often. The current versions could also be downloaded and tried for free for 90 days. The trial period was never really enforced, however, and so many got Netscape for free that way. There was also a version that consumers could mail order, which provided some income. Andreesen and the others did not worry so much about making money selling the browser. If everyone was using it, they could make money in other ways, such as selling advertising on their home page.

On October 13, 1994, Mosaic Netscape was posted for download on the Internet. Within weeks it was the browser of choice for the majority of Web users. It included new HTML tags that allowed Web designers greater control and creativity. Excited designers quickly began incorporating the new tags into their pages. These could only be read by Netscape, so the designers would usually include a note that their pages were best viewed with Netscape and a link to the page where it could be downloaded. This was great advertising for Netscape. It also further grew the Web itself because Web pages became more exciting.

There was one major problem facing Mosaic. The University of Illinois claimed that Mosaic Netscape had stolen Mosaic from them and demanded they change their name and quit distributing their product. Mosaic changed their name to Netscape Communications Corporation, but refused to quit distributing their software. On December 21, 1994, an agreement was reached. The University of Illinois made no further claims on Netscape and received a financial settlement. This, plus legal expenses, cost Netscape close to $3mn. Good news had come just six days earlier when the shipping versions of Netscape were ready for distribution, which brought in some actual income.

Perhaps as much can be learned from Netscape's downfall as from its meteoric rise to the top. By 1996, 75% of Web users used Netscape. Now it is merely a subsidiary of America Online and has only a third of the Web's users. Microsoft Internet Explorer has replaced Netscape as browser number one.

What happened? Surely, part of the reason for the dramatic change of fortune for Netscape is that Microsoft is simply too strong a competitor (ongoing legal battles will determine whether they are actually a monopoly). But some believe bad management at Netscape also contributed to its downfall. They point to a "Just show up" strategy for success. Netscape management saw its product as superior and looking at its huge share of the market rested on their laurels to some degree. Over time, Internet Explorer became the more reliable browser with better features. Netscape continued to charge for its product; its pricing structure continually changed and was inconsistent, while Internet Explorer has always been totally free.

By 1999, Netscape was battle-weary, and America Online bought it for $10bn in stock. America Online does not use Navigator as its official browser. It does not seem interested in Netscape software, but rather in converting the remaining Netscape audience into its own.

The new marketplace of the World Wide Web is a very volatile and dynamic one. Getting to the top is difficult, but staying there is even harder. In an environment that changes so rapidly it would seem that competitors too would have to be willing and able to change continuously.

BERNERS-LEE, TIM

Tim graduated from the Queen's College at Oxford University, England, 1976. While there he built his first computer with a soldering iron, TTL gates, an M6800 processor and an old television.

He spent two years with Plessey Telecommunications Ltd (Poole, Dorset, UK) a major UK telecom equipment manufacturer, working on distributed transaction systems, message relays, and bar code technology.

In 1978 Tim left Plessey to join D.G. Nash Ltd (Ferndown, Dorset, UK), where he wrote among other things typesetting software for intelligent printers and a multitasking operating system.

A year and a half spent as an independent consultant included a six-month stint (Jun–Dec 1980) as consultant software engineer at CERN, the European Particle Physics Laboratory in Geneva, Switzerland. While there, he wrote for his own private use his first program for storing information including using random associations. Named "Enquire," and never published, this program formed the conceptual basis for the future development of the World Wide Web.

From 1981 until 1984, Tim worked at John Poole's Image Computer Systems Ltd, with technical design responsibility. Work here included real-time control firmware, graphics and communications software, and a generic macro language. In 1984, he took up a fellowship at CERN, to work on distributed real-time systems for scientific data acquisition and system control. Among other things, he worked on FASTBUS system software and designed a heterogeneous remote procedure call system.

In 1989, he proposed a global hypertext project, to be known as the World Wide Web. Based on the earlier "Enquire" work, it was designed to allow people to work together by combining their knowledge in a web of hypertext documents. He wrote the first World Wide Web server, "httpd," and the first client, "WorldWideWeb" – a what-you-see-is-what-you-get hypertext browser/editor which ran in the NeXTStep environment. This work was started in October 1990, and the program "WorldWideWeb" was first made available within CERN in December, and on the Internet at large in the summer of 1991.

Through 1991 and 1993, Tim continued working on the design of the Web, co-ordinating feedback from users across the Internet. His initial specifications of URLs, HTTP and HTML were refined and discussed in larger circles as the Web technology spread.

In 1994, Tim joined the Laboratory for Computer Science (LCS) at the Massachusetts Institute of Technology (MIT). In 1999, he became the first holder of the 3Com founders chair. He is director of the World Wide

Web Consortium, which coordinates Web development worldwide, with teams at MIT, at the Institut National de Recherche en Informatique et en Automatique in France, and at Keio University in Japan. The Consortium takes as its goal to lead the Web to its full potential, ensuring its stability through rapid evolution and revolutionary transformations of its usage.

CERF, VINT

As a graduate student at UCLA, Vint Cerf was involved in the early design of the ARPANET. He was present when the first IMP was delivered to UCLA. He is called the "father of the Internet." He earned this nickname as one of the co-authors of TCP/IP – the protocol that allowed ARPA to connect various independent networks together to form one large network of networks – the Internet.

When Cerf graduated from Stanford in 1965, he went to work for IBM as a systems engineer, but soon decided to return to school to learn more about computers. He enrolled in UCLA's computer science department and began pursuing his Ph.D. His thesis was based on work he did on an ARPA-funded project for the "Snuper Computer" – a computer that was designed to observe remotely the execution of programs on another computer.

The Snuper Computer project got Cerf interested in the field of computer networking. In the fall of 1968, ARPA set up another program at UCLA in anticipation of building the ARPANET, called the Network Measurement Center. It was responsible for performance testing and analysis, a sort of testing ground. Len Kleinrock managed about 40 students who ran the center. Cerf was one of the senior members of the team.

By the end of 1968, a small group of graduate students from the four schools that were slated to be the first four nodes on the ARPANET (UCLA, Stanford Research Institute (SRI), the University of Utah, and UCSB) began meeting regularly to discuss the new network and problems related to its development. They called themselves the Network Working Group (NWG), and although NWG proved to be instrumental in solving many of the problems that would arrive during the design and implementation of the ARPANET, its members did not realize their importance at the time. Cerf recalls:

"We were just rank amateurs, and we were expecting that some authority would finally come along and say, 'Here's how we are going to do it.' And nobody ever came along."

One of the main obstacles facing the deployment of ARPA's network was the problem of getting incompatible host computers to communicate with one another through the Interface Message Processor (IMP). Bolt Beranek & Newman (BBN) was only responsible for building the IMPs and making sure they could move packets, not devising the methods they and the host computers would use to communicate. Devising standards for communication, what came to be known as a protocol, became one of the NWG's main tasks.

The NWG implemented a "layered" approach in building a protocol. This means that they created several simple "building block" protocols that could later be joined to oversee network communication as a whole. In 1970, the group released a protocol for basic host-to-host communication called the Network Control Protocol (NCP). They also created several other protocols to work on top of NCP such as Telnet, which allowed for remote logins.

In August 1969, BBN delivered the first IMP to UCLA. A month later the second was delivered to SRI, and the ARPANET continued to grow quickly from that point. Cerf was present when the first IMP was delivered to UCLA, and was involved with the IMP immediately, performing various tests on the new hardware. It was during this testing that he met Bob Kahn, with whom he enjoyed a good working relationship.

Within a few years of the creation of the ARPANET, other computer networks were deployed. They were all independent, self-contained networks. Cerf recalls:

"Around this time Bob started saying, 'Look, my problem is how I get a computer that's on a satellite and a computer on a radio net and a computer on ARPANET to communicate uniformly with each other without realizing what's going on in between?'"

They decided that there needed to be a "gateway" computer between each network to route packets. The gateway computers would not care about the various complexities of each network. They would simply be in charge of passing packets back and forth. But all of the networks transmitted packets in different ways, using their own protocols. A new standard was needed to link all of the networks and allow inter-network communication.

Cerf and Kahn began working out a plan in 1973. In September, they presented a paper outlining their ideas to the International Networking Group.

In May 1974, they completed their paper entitled *A Protocol for Packet Network Intercommunication.* They described a new protocol they called the Transmission Control Protocol (TCP), in which the main idea was to enclose packets in "datagrams." These were to act something like envelopes containing letters. The content and format of the letter is not important for its delivery – the information on the envelope is standardized to facilitate delivery. Gateway computers would simply read only the delivery information contained in the datagrams and deliver the contents to host computers. Only the host computers would actually "open" the envelope and read the actual contents of the packet. TCP allowed networks to be joined into a network of networks, or what we now call the Internet.

Cerf continued to refine TCP. In 1976, he accepted a job as program manager responsible for what was then called the "ARPA Internet" at ARPA. In 1978 he and several of his colleagues made a major refinement by splitting TCP into two parts. They took the part of TCP that is responsible for routing packages and formed a separate protocol called the Internet Protocol (IP). TCP would remain responsible for dividing messages into datagrams, reassembling messages, detecting errors, putting packets in the right order, and resending lost packets. The new protocol was called TCP/IP, and it went on to become the standard for all Internet communication.

Today Cerf is the chief Internet strategist for WorldCom. His latest pet project is called the Interplanetary Network (IPN). This project, part of NASA's Jet Propulsion Laboratory, will basically extend the Internet into outer space.

KLEINROCK, DR LEONARD

Dr Kleinrock is known as the Inventor of the Internet Technology, having created the basic principles of packet switching (the technology underpinning the Internet) while a graduate student at MIT. This was a decade before the birth of the Internet, which occurred when his host computer at UCLA became the first node of the Internet in September 1969. He wrote the first paper and published the first book on the subject; he also directed the transmission of the first message ever to pass over the Internet.

Dr Kleinrock received his Ph.D. from MIT in 1963 and has served as a professor of computer science at the University of California, Los Angeles since then. He received his BEE degree from CCNY in 1957, also honorary doctorates of science from CCNY in 1997, and from the University of Massachusetts, Amherst in 2000. He is a co-founder of Linkabit; also founder and chairman of Nomadix, Inc. and of Technology Transfer Institute; both high tech firms located in Santa Monica, CA. He has published more than 200 papers and authored six books on a wide array of subjects including packet switching networks, packet radio networks, local area networks, broadband networks and gigabit networks. Additionally, Dr Kleinrock has recently launched the field of nomadic computing, the emerging technology to support users as soon as they leave their desktop environments; nomadic computing may well be the next major wave of the Internet.

He is a member of the National Academy of Engineering, an IEEE fellow, an ACM fellow and a founding member of the Computer Science and Telecommunications Board of the National Research Council. Among his many honors, he is the recipient of the CCNY Townsend Harris Medal, the CCNY Electrical Engineering Award, the Marconi Award, the L.M. Ericsson Prize, the NAE Charles Stark Draper Prize, the IEEE Internet Millennium Award, the UCLA Outstanding Teacher Award, the Lanchester Prize, the ACM SIGCOMM Award, the Sigma Xi Monie Ferst Award, the INFORMS Presidents Award, and the IEEE Harry Goode Award.

He first became interested in electronics at the age of six while reading a comic book in which the centerfold described how to build a crystal radio. He managed to collect the parts, make it work, and was amazed to hear music from this simple device; thus was an engineer born. The rest is history.

METCALFE, BOB

As a graduate student, Bob Metcalfe worked on the ARPANET at MIT. He later developed a new technology, called Ethernet, for connecting computers in a local network.

Metcalfe was born in 1946, in Brooklyn, NY. He attended MIT where he earned degrees in electrical engineering and business management. He then earned a master's degree in applied mathematics from Harvard. While working on his Ph.D. in computer science at Harvard, he took a job at MIT building the hardware that would link MIT to the ARPANET. For a 1972 ARPANET conference he wrote an introductory pamphlet entitled *Scenarios*. It included 19 scenarios for using the ARPANET, listed available resources at the various sites, and basic usage instructions.

Metcalfe had done a good job writing his informative booklet and was chosen to take ten AT&T officials on a virtual tour of the network. Unfortunately, the system crashed while Metcalfe was giving his demonstration. Metcalfe said:

> "I looked up in pain and I caught them smiling, delighted that packet-switching was flaky. This I will never forget. It confirmed for them that circuit-switching technology was here to stay, and this packet-switching stuff was an unreliable toy that would never have much impact in the commercial world. It was clear to me they were tangled in the past."

Metcalfe's unpleasant experience with the AT&T officials made a lasting impression. Said Metcalfe:

> "I saw that there are people who will connive against innovation. They're hostile to it. And that has shaped my behavior ever since."

Metcalfe was excited about the ARPANET and made it the topic of his doctoral dissertation. He was shocked when Harvard flunked him. His dissertation was "not theoretical enough." Metcalfe was angry:

"They let me go into this thing and they gunned me. I'm even willing to stipulate that it wasn't very good. But I'd still justify my anger at those bastards for letting me fail. Had they been doing better jobs as professors, they would never have allowed that to happen. But I hated Harvard and Harvard hated me. It was a class thing from the start."

Having already accepted a job at Xerox's Palo Alto Research Center (PARC), he was told to come take his job anyway and finish his doctoral work later. His inspiration for a new dissertation came when he read a paper about the ALOHA network, or Alohanet, at the University of Hawaii. The Alohanet used radio waves instead of telephone wire to transmit data. The main problem with using radio waves as a medium was that if two packets were sent out at the same time on the same broadcast channel they would interfere with each other and effectively cut off the transmission.

The Alohanet designers implemented a method called random access. Computers were allowed to transmit whenever they had data to send. They then waited to receive confirmation from the destination computer that the packets arrived. If packets collided and no confirmation was received, the sending computer would wait for a random (but very short) period of time and retransmit.

Metcalfe saw several problems in the design. He reworked it, and made it the topic of his new dissertation. His key improvement was to vary the random interval for re-transmission based on traffic load. If there was a lot of data traffic, the computer would wait longer periods before retransmitting. This would greatly improve efficiency by limiting the number of repeat collisions. Metcalfe's new dissertation was accepted and he finally got his Ph.D.

Back at Xerox PARC, Metcalfe was given the task of designing a way to connect their new personal computers, the Altos, to each other. He modified his version of the Alohanet to use cables instead of radio, and with several other adjustments created a new technology he called Ethernet. This worked well, and Metcalfe started what would be years of selling his invention. In 1979, he started his own company, 3Com (which stands for computers, communication, compatibility) and continued to push Ethernet as the new standard for local area networks (LANs).

Throughout the 1980s LANs became very popular. They were especially popular at universities where many workstations were connected using Ethernet. Those LANs were in turn connected to the Internet to facilitate inter-institution communication. In this way, Ethernet was influential in the expansion of the Internet.

09

Resources

There are many useful resources on the Internet and business. This chapter identifies the best books on the topic.

Berners-Lee, Tim with Mark Fischetti, *Weaving the Web: The Original Design and Ultimate Destiny of the World Wide Web, by its Inventor* (HarperCollins, 1999)

This book is written to address the questions most people ask – from "What were you thinking when you invented it?" through "So what do you think of it now?" to "Where is this all going to take us?" – this is the story. It is not a technical book. It does mention a little about how technologies you may have heard of – like XML – fit into the past, present and future, but only in the process of charting a course for the Web from the initial dream – still largely unfulfilled – to the next technical and social revolution.

Cohan, Peter, *E-Profit: High-Payoff Strategies for Capturing the E-Commerce Edge* (AMACOM, 2000)

E-Profit evaluates getting into e-business, covering topics such as the economic benefits of e-commerce, safety and privacy concerns, the AOL–Time Warner merger, day trading and the investment possibilities of the Internet, predictions of the hottest e-businesses currently on the horizon and the future trends in electronic commerce.

Cohan, Peter, *Net Profit: How to Invest and Compete in the Real World of Internet Business* (Jossey-Bass, 1999)

The bulk of this work consists of an economic evaluation of nine Internet business segments, including Powerware, Brandware, and Lossware businesses. After defining the segments, business consultant Cohan analyzes their markets and profit potentials, presents case studies, and describes the implications for managers. Finally, he applies the lessons to non-Internet businesses' decisions to sell on the Web.

Downes, Larry; Mui, Chunka; Negroponte, Nicholas, *Unleashing the Killer App: Digital Strategies for Market Dominance* (Harvard Business School Press, 2000)

In *Unleashing the Killer App*, authors Downes, Mui, and Negroponte look at the dynamics of technological change and its potential to create "killer apps." The authors describe a killer app as a product or service that:

> "wind[s] up displacing unrelated older offerings, destroying and re-creating industries far from their immediate use, and throwing into disarray the complex relationships between business partners, competitors, customers, and regulators of markets."

Examples of killer apps throughout history include the Welsh longbow, the pulley, the compass, movable type, and the Apple Macintosh. And today, with our increasingly networked economy (for example, the World Wide Web), killer apps are appearing all around us.

Downes and Mui argue that the dominant trend behind the proliferation of killer apps is a combination of Moore's Law, which states that the processing power of the Central Processing Unit (CPU) doubles every 18 months, and Metcalfe's Law, which observes that the value of a network increases dramatically with each node that is added to it. These two laws are fundamentally changing how businesses interact with each other and with their customers. To exploit these changes, the authors outline 12 points for designing a digital strategy to help you identify and create killer apps in your own organization. The book includes dozens of examples of how killer apps were discovered and implemented.

Kelly, Kevin, *New Rules for the New Economy: 10 Radical Strategies for a Connected World* (Penguin USA, 1999)

Kevin Kelly has long been one of the new economy's chief hypesters. In *New Rules for the New Economy*, he tries to encapsulate the characteristics of this emerging economic order by laying out 10 rules for how the wired world operates. The result is a look at the behavior of networks and their effect on our economic lives.

At the root of this network revolution is communication. Kelly synthesizes large amounts of information in unique and interesting ways. His ability to turn a phrase is reflected in the names he gives to his 10 rules, and it makes this book a pleasure to read. Some, for example, are:

» Embrace the Swarm: The Power of Decentralization (Rule 1);
» No Harmony, All Flux: Seeking Sustainable Disequilibrium (Rule 8); and
» Let Go at the Top: After Success, Devolution'' (Rule 6).

A few of his ideas are elusive and difficult to evaluate.

Mandel, Michael, *The Coming Internet Depression: Why the High-Tech Boom Will Go Bust, Why the Crash Will Be Worse Than You Think, and How to Prosper Afterward* (Basic Books, 2000)

Michael J. Mandel begins *The Coming Internet Depression* by explaining why just such a depression is not only possible but increasingly likely. His explanation is based on a comparison of the present period with the 1920s: both saw tremendous growth in GDP that was largely centered on the "hypergrowth" of a single industry – automobiles in the 1920s, information technology today. When this "hypergrowth" reverts to a normal growth pattern, as the automobile industry did in 1929, the resulting overcapacity will slow down the entire economy.

Mandel addresses three key questions: When will the Internet Depression start? How will we know when it's coming? How bad will it be? Finally, he shows how investors, workers, and businesses can navigate the bad times safely and prosper in the long recovery that will follow.

Modahl, Mary, *Now or Never: How Companies Must Change Today to Win the Battle for Internet Consumers* (HarperBusiness, 1999)

In *Now or Never*, Mary Modahl argues that we are in the first year of a "ten year transition in the way consumers shop and save," and that winning in the Internet space not only requires identifying consumers that are most likely to take their shopping online, but exploiting the new and different business models made possible by online commerce.

Modahl believes that conventional demographics, which segment populations according to their income and education, is a poor predictor of online behavior. As an alternative, she advances Forrester Research's work on "technographics," which measure consumers' attitudes toward technology. Forrester has found that 52% of the population is optimistic about technology and is "matching happily towards online shopping," and she shows how companies can better target their marketing strategies to meet this growing legion of consumers.

In addition, Modahl considers the "post-Internet competitive environment," which she thinks will be "far more fluid and responsive to changes in supply and demand." Using examples of traditional industries that have had their business models turned upside down by Internet economies – newspapers, travel agencies, and brokerages – Modahl offers ways in which the old guard can better cope with technology change, channel conflict, and their own inertia toward this new marketplace.

Perkins, Anthony; Perkins, Michael, *The Internet Bubble: Inside the Overvalued World of High-Tech Stocks – and What You Need to Know to Avoid the Coming Shakeout* (HarperBusiness, 1999)

Canals. Railroads. Automobiles. Computers. The Internet. Each represented revolutionary shifts in the way Americans would live and do business. Each saw a corresponding rush of investors to get in on the great new investment opportunity. Each saw a lot of investors go broke.

In *The Internet Bubble*, Anthony and Michael Perkins, founding editors of *Red Herring*, look at it this way: in the early twentieth century, there were more than 500 automobile companies in the US. Now how many are there? Same with the new Internet companies, the Perkins's predict. A few will grow into profitable businesses in 10 or 20 years, but even then, their stocks may not be worth much more than their 1999 prices. They argue that buying an Internet stock today is really nothing more than gambling that someone else will come along and buy it from you for more money.

The book includes an overview of the biggest players in the Internet explosion, the market mania for Internet stocks, and profiles of companies such as Amazon.com, Yahoo!, and At Home. The authors also interview venture capitalists who help new companies get off the ground and the investment bankers who help them go public. And while they don't pretend that they know when the Internet bubble will burst, or what the damage will be, they are convinced that most dot-com companies will never make a dime.

The authors conclude with some thoughts about investing in this climate, and argue that ignoring the Internet may be as dangerous to your portfolio as investing too much. Some guidelines about product cycles and diversification appear, but the biggest rule seems to be: don't be the one holding the hot potato at the end of the game.

Schwartz, Evan, *Digital Darwinism: 7 Breakthrough Business Strategies for Surviving in the Cut-throat Web Economy* (Broadway Books, 1999)

Evan I. Schwartz tries to discover the characteristics of the Internet winners that will eventually emerge. In *Digital Darwinism*, he identifies seven strategies that will separate the winners from the losers. These include building a brand that stands for solving something, elastic pricing, affiliate partnerships, and integrating digital commerce with every aspect of business.

Schwartz buttresses his arguments with analyses of dozens of companies already competing on the Internet, including Yahoo!, Peapod, Priceline, E*Trade, Dell Computer, and Recreational Equipment, Inc. He views these early years of the Web as largely "irrational," but anticipates a general rationalization. He writes:

"As each successive generation of Web commerce passes, there will be more rational companies and fewer irrational ones, more fit business models and fewer unfit ones. In the future, there may be no such thing as an Internet company. The Internet is becoming so important that all companies will eventually become Internet companies."

Seybold, Patricia, *Customers.com: How to Create a Profitable Business Strategy for the Internet & Beyond* (Times Books, 1998)

Drawing on case studies of companies and organizations such as Boeing, Babson College, National Semiconductor, Hertz, PhotoDisc, and Wells Fargo, Seybold identifies what makes e-commerce work successfully. She argues that any e-commerce initiative has to begin with the customer.

The first section of the book outlines five steps aimed at any organization grappling with the challenge of doing e-commerce right. The final section offers a technology roadmap and suggestions for getting e-commerce initiatives off the ground. But at the heart of the book are 16 case studies of companies that have successfully embraced e-business and e-commerce. Each is well researched, includes an executive summary, and "take-aways" about what each firm did right.

Shapiro, Carl; Varian, Hal, *Information Rules: A Strategic Guide to the Network Economy* (Harvard Business School Press, 1998)

Chapter 1 of *Information Rules* begins with a description of the change brought on by technology at the close of the century – but the century described is not this one, it's the late 1800s. One hundred years ago, it was an emerging telephone and electrical network that was transforming business. Today it's the Internet. The point? While the circumstances of a particular era may be unique, the underlying principles that describe the exchange of goods in a free-market economy are the same.

Carl Shapiro and Hal Varian offer a deep knowledge of how economic systems work coupled with first-hand experience of today's network economy. Shapiro and Varian consider how to market and distribute goods in the network economy, citing examples from industries as diverse as airlines, software, entertainment, and communications. The authors cover issues such as pricing, intellectual property, versioning, lock-in, compatibility, and standards.

Tapscott, Don, *Digital Capital: Harnessing the Power of Business Webs* (Harvard Business School Publishing, 2000)

Business webs (b-webs) are partner networks of producers, service providers, suppliers, infrastructure companies, and customers linked via digital channels. This book describes the b-web phenomenon and the five types of b-web now in play: agoras, aggregations, value chains, alliances, and distributive networks.

Ten Steps to Making it Work

Putting the management secrets of the e-leaders into practice is easier said than done. This final chapter helps managers adapt their organizations to achieve the performance-enhancing characteristics of technology leaders by covering the following steps:

1. build Web application team;
2. set objectives;
3. benchmark peers;
4. work with customers and suppliers;
5. map current processes;
6. envision new Web application;
7. design new processes and systems;
8. sell senior management;
9. roll out in phases; and
10. measure, evaluate, and improve.

Once a firm has decided to proceed with a Web application, management needs to make change happen in order to achieve the desired results. The managerial steps will vary by project. Level I projects, for example, may not require as much process redesign work as Level III projects. Therefore, managers will need to evaluate what steps are appropriate for their particular project. Here is a relatively comprehensive ten-step process that managers can follow to realize the potential of their Web application.

1. BUILD WEB APPLICATION TEAM

To ensure success, the Web application must be led from the top. The leader is likely to be the CEO in a small organization and a business unit manager in a medium- or large-sized organization. The leader must form a cross-functional team and offer tangible incentives to motivate its drive to success. The team must be trained in the techniques it will need to do an effective job of Web-enabled process redesign. The team should consist of business unit managers, functional managers, and IS professionals. External stakeholders – such as customers and suppliers – should participate on the team where needed. The leader should direct a steering committee that offers advice and keeps the project on track.

2. SET OBJECTIVES

The leader must set objectives for the Web application team. These objectives should be specific, measurable, ambitious, and yet achievable. Web applications cannot be considered a success until they have produced measurable performance improvements in areas such as enhanced customer service, better quality, faster response time, and lower costs. As we mentioned earlier, setting big objectives is useful. However, the team should organize its work to achieve measurable results quickly rather than working on an ambitious project for 24 to 36 months with the hope of achieving the big results at the end.

3. BENCHMARK PEERS

The Web application team should identify other companies that have done similar Web applications. These benchmark companies should be within the industry and outside it. The benchmarking efforts should be highly focused on generating insights into what works and what does not work in process redesign.

4. WORK WITH CUSTOMERS AND SUPPLIERS

The Web application team should also work closely with relevant customers and suppliers. In particular, the team should find out what these stakeholders like about the current processes and where they see opportunities for improvement. Working with customers and suppliers helps the Web application team create a new process that benefits these stakeholders.

5. MAP CURRENT PROCESSES

The Web application team must then map the processes that are to be changed. Process mapping pays off by identifying opportunities for improvement. The Web application team can compare the insights from process mapping with the complaints of customers and suppliers, and with the effective techniques of the benchmark companies. Areas where all three of these analyses overlap are likely to contain the greatest potential for providing meaningful results.

6. ENVISION NEW WEB APPLICATION

Once the team has collected all this data, it must envision a new Web application that will be radical enough to produce big performance improvement but practical enough to be achievable. In order to achieve this, all members of the team must review the results of the foregoing analytical steps.

Then the team should brainstorm to develop ideas about what a new process would look like. Initially, the team should strive to generate a large number of new ideas, and then criteria for ranking them. Criteria for ranking a process might include its ability to achieve management objectives, its cost and time to implement, its ability to use much existing data, processes and systems, etc. The team should rank the ideas based on these criteria and then pick the best of the group.

7. DESIGN NEW PROCESSES AND SYSTEMS

The team must now shift its focus to designing new workflows, new performance incentives, and new information systems. All of these processes and systems must work together for re-engineering to succeed. The team will work with affected people throughout the organization, both internal departments and external stakeholders. Working with these people, the team will design new ways that people will work together. The team will envision how performance measurement and incentives must change. And the team will design the new Web application that will support the new work processes.

8. SELL SENIOR MANAGEMENT

At this point, the team has reached the point where it will need to request resources from senior management. To do so, it will need to develop the business case for the project. The case should help persuade senior management that the resources required for the project will be more than offset by the benefits that the Web application will produce for the company. The business case should include specific project objectives, a description of the benefits that the project will produce for the firm, highlights of how the new process will differ from the old one, an overview of the technical architecture of the new system, a project plan, and the anticipated budget required to achieve the plan.

If management approves the business case, then the team should present a detailed implementation plan to senior management and get their advice and consent to proceed with the project. An important part of the implementation plan is the process of evaluating and selecting potential suppliers of Web tools and systems integration services for building the application. Given the importance of these inputs to the project, the team may decide to select suppliers before seeking the CEO's final approval of the project.

9. ROLL OUT IN PHASES

As Pete Solvik, architect of Cisco's CCO recommends, teams should break a project into discrete phases that take no more than 90 days to complete. Each of these brief project phases should add a specific feature that is likely to produce measurable benefits. If the project phases actually achieve the anticipated benefits, then management will feel much more comfortable in continuing to fund the project. The team should start with project phases that are most likely to generate big results quickly in order to build enthusiasm for the project.

10. MEASURE, EVALUATE, AND IMPROVE

Finally, the CEO should recognize that the Web application process never really ends. The firm should evaluate the quantitative benefit of the project in relation to its ongoing costs. External and internal stakeholders of the Web application should provide feedback to the company to identify what works and what needs improvement. Even after completion, new technologies are likely to emerge that could be incorporated into the system to make it more effective or efficient.

Frequently Asked Questions (FAQs)

Q1: Who are the e-leaders?

A: See Chapter 2.

Q2: Why are the e-leaders important?

A: See Chapter 1.

Q3: What are the nine Internet business segments?

A: See Chapter 2.

Q4: How can an investor pick the best segments and companies within those segments?

A: See Chapter 2.

Q5: How should a "land-based" company best use the Internet to enhance its profits?

A: See Chapter 5.

Q6: What is the history of the Internet?

A: See Chapter 3.

Q7: Who are the leading thinkers in the evolution of the Internet?

A: See Chapter 8.

Q8: What are the current issues in e-business?

A: See Chapter 6.

Q9: How do I find out more about the subject?

A: See Chapter 9.

Q10: What can my organization do better as a result of the lessons from the e-leaders?

A: See Chapter 10.

Index

Printed and bound by CPI Group (UK) Ltd, Croydon, CR0 4YY

13/04/2025

14656458-0004